GOING BOHEMIAN

Activities That Engage Adolescents in the Art of Writing Well

Lawrence Baines
Berry College
Mount Berry, Georgia, USA

Anthony J. Kunkel
Rome High School
Rome, Georgia, USA

Editors

INTERNATIONAL
Reading
Association

800 Barksdale Road, PO Box 8139
Newark, Delaware 19714-8139, USA
www.reading.org

The International Reading Association attempts, through its publications, to provide a forum for a wide spectrum of opinions on reading. This policy permits divergent viewpoints without implying the endorsement of the Association.

Director of Publications   Joan M. Irwin
Assistant Director of Publications   Jeanette K. Moss
Editor in Chief, Books   Matthew W. Baker
Permissions Editor   Janet S. Parrack
Associate Editor   Tori Mello
Assistant Editor   Sarah Rutigliano
Acquisitions and Communications Coordinator   Amy T. Roff
Publications Coordinator   Beth Doughty
Association Editor   David K. Roberts
Production Department Manager   Iona Sauscermen
Art Director   Boni Nash
Electronic Publishing Supervisor   Wendy A. Mazur
Electronic Publishing Specialist   Anette Schütz-Ruff
Electronic Publishing Specialist   Cheryl J. Strum
Electronic Publishing Assistant   Peggy Mason

Project Editor   Tori Mello

Cover Design   Boni Nash

CONTENTS

Contributors

Lesley Atwater
English teacher
Orange Grove Middle School
Tampa, Florida, USA

Coleen Baines
former English teacher
Rome, Georgia, USA

Lawrence Baines
Green Endowed Chair in Education
Berry College
Mount Berry, Georgia, USA

Pamela Sissi Carroll
Associate Professor of English Education
Florida State University
Tallahassee, Florida, USA

Robert Kohser
English teacher
Dixie County High School
Cross City, Florida, USA

Anthony Kunkel
English teacher
Rome High School
Rome, Georgia, USA

Sydeana Martin
English teacher
Tallahassee, Florida, USA

Jan Miller
Science teacher
Chattooga High School
Summerville, Georgia, USA

Barbara Moore
English teacher
Ocala, Florida, USA

Alan Perry
English teacher
Chattooga High School
Summerville, Georgia, USA

Tracie Pullum
English teacher
Miami Lakes Middle School
Miami, Florida, USA

Mike Rychlik
English teacher
School for Applied Individualized Learning
Tallahassee, Florida, USA

Irving Seidman
Professor
University of Massachusetts at Amherst
School of Education
Amherst, Massachusetts, USA

Greg Stanley
Social Studies teacher
Rome High School
Rome, Georgia, USA

Tom Stewart
English teacher
Butler County Middle School
Morgantown, Kentucky, USA

Blake Tenore
English teacher
Kannapolis, North Carolina, USA

Cara Turner
Doctoral student
Secondary Teacher Education
University of Massachusetts at Amherst
Amherst, Massachusetts, USA

Wendy Vascik
English teacher
San Marino, California, USA

Hannah Walker
Middle grades major
Berry College
Mount Berry, Georgia, USA

Clarissa West-White
Doctoral student
English Education
Florida State University
Tallahassee, Florida, USA

Going Bohemian

CHANCES ARE THAT MOST SCHOOLS HAVE ONE OR TWO. Although they don't always fit the mold of the traditional faculty member, they seem to click with students, at times making connections with adolescents who had been considered beyond redemption. These teachers seem to enjoy spurning traditional teaching methods in favor of establishing an "artsy," intense, and engaging classroom environment. Sometimes their creative energies come off as purposefully radical or unnecessarily hyperactive, but their classrooms are never dull. A colleague once characterized such teachers as "fringe-dwellers" because they always seem to be dancing on the edge of acceptability within the school culture.

At some schools, these individuals are called "beasties" or "Bohemians" because their penchant for living as artists or poets creeps into the very fabric of their teaching. According to the dictionary, a Bohemian is one "who lives in an unconventional, nonconforming way" (Neufelt, 1994). Bohemian teachers are often the topic of lunchroom discussions and rumors emanating from the faculty lounge. Feared by some colleagues, envied by others, these Bohemians are nevertheless held in high regard by students who appreciate that they accept nothing short of their students' best efforts.

Many non-Bohemian teachers approach the teaching of writing like they think they are supposed to—with loads of journal writing and free writing, little teacher intrusion, and a grading system that emphasizes effort over product. Composition lessons are built around district curriculum guides, available textbooks, and the suggestions of the head of the department. Long-term goals are planned meticulously, a set of materials needed for the year is lined up, and a clear explanation of grading procedures is distributed to students and administrators. Indeed, it is the contention of most textbooks on classroom discipline that the tone for the academic year should be set within the first week:

"Read page 12, do questions 1 through 9, then choose one of the essay prompts."

Using such an approach in a classroom seems to result in a familiar pattern: A percentage of students do their work unobtrusively, another group seems to struggle and complain about every little assignment, while many others—even the most capable—show little interest in anything. Unfortunately, academic work is often perceived by adolescents as a kind of never-never-land that is guided by nothing more than the whims and demands of idiosyncratic teachers and the minimal demands of the state. All that is learned is considered to be of little value outside of the classroom. When students begin to display oppositional behaviors, a teacher will often chastise them by admonishing, "You need to know how to do this next year when you are a _____ (freshman in college, senior, junior, sophomore, freshman, eighth-grader, seventh-grader)."

Of course, most teachers want to do the right things: They want students to complete the kinds of language arts assignments that they consider valuable; but after being confronted by that inevitable sea of blank stares day after day, even the most positive teachers can eventually convince themselves that "students just don't care."

After teaching for a few years and becoming thoroughly underwhelmed with the results we were getting, we each did a little self-analysis. Eventually we arrived at the conclusion that not only were we ineffective teachers, we would have despised our own classes if we had been unfortunate enough to have been enrolled in them. We discovered that we had built our classrooms on the innumerable suggestions of strangers and their lists of books titles, standards, and competencies. We had heeded their advice without ever considering our own talents or those of the students we taught.

So we decided to go Bohemian—to trust our individual muses, to begin using activities that really worked in class rather than attempting to align our practice with a trendy theoretical stance or state mandate. In short, we became teachers again. We stopped trying to please everybody, we intensified instruction, and we started demanding total participation from students. We began using only those activities that would engage and educate students, built on those, and let go of the dull and superficial paeans to bureaucracy. Students whined, cried, laughed, shouted, and wrote until their hands ached.

Gradually, we found other Bohemian teachers who were willing to trade lesson plans and samples of student work. We tried their lessons in our classrooms, kept them if they worked, and adapted or deleted them if they didn't. *Going Bohemian: Activities That Engage Adolescents in the Art of Writing Well* is a collection of the "keepers"—those lesson plans that always seemed to work for us and our Bohemian compadres.

The activities in *Going Bohemian* often advocate using off-beat strategies, competitive games, interdisciplinary hooks, art and multimedia, and indirect approaches to teaching some of the difficult lessons of writing. Rather than employing a strictly collaborative or teacher-dominated approach, Bohemian lesson plans use "interestingness" as the entry point for student participation. Once students become immersed in doing these activities, they seem to take off on their own. However, the success of any of these lessons depends on the role of the teacher as evaluator, organizer, helper, cheerleader, disciplinarian, and writer. The Bohemian teacher is no guide on the side, but is a charismatic, demanding artist who expects students to create papers and performances that are meaningful, lively, fresh, and beautifully rendered.

Organization of the Book

Going Bohemian begins with an unexpurgated essay from a student concerning the differences between a teacher who has gone Bohemian and one who is only going through the motions. From there, the book is divided into nine sections, each containing five writing activities. A short narrative introducing each section includes a table that briefly describes each activity by title, entry point, skills it helps develop, and the amount of preparation time necessary to do the activity in class. The entry point is the lure used to initially engage students, which might be anything from a piece of classical music to a field trip to a local cemetery. The specific skill being addressed by the activity is listed under the heading "students develop." The amount of preparation time is categorized as being either minimal (under 10 minutes) or substantial (somewhere between 10 minutes and 2 weeks). These categories allow teachers who need a quick activity to locate one without having to read through the entire book. The activities themselves are presented in a format that attempts to be teacher friendly and easy to follow, with sections on objectives, materials, set-up, procedures, summary, and enrichment. Best of all, many of the activities are accompanied by a student sample. We also have included a resources appendix, which lists all books, magazines, music, and films mentioned throughout the activities.

Section One describes activities that would be appropriate at the beginning of the year for teachers who want to get to know their students, to learn the range of their writing abilities, and to establish the classroom as an intellectually stimulating place to be. Section Two contains activities that use film, the Internet, performance, newscasts, and presentation software in the cause of the written word. Indicative of the content of this section is the activity "Pop-Up Videos," in which instead of viewing music videos as the enemy, Leslie Atwater shows how a teacher can use them to teach students some research skills as well as some fundamentals of punctuation and grammar.

Upon reading a preliminary draft of the manuscript for this book, one non-Bohemian teacher remarked, "But you can't always make learning fun. Try making parts of speech and constructing effective sentences fun." Section Three was created expressly to demonstrate that even the most seemingly dry activity can be made stimulating and inviting. Whether students are attempting to solve the word puzzle of "Scrambled Sentences" or sleuthing for words that might be adjectives, students often become so engaged in these activities that they don't realize that they are learning fundamentals of grammar and composition. Enhancing the vocabularies of students is also an objective for the activities in Section Four, "Enriching Vocabulary." When his classes play "Vocab War," some of Anthony Kunkel's students have been known to get so competitive that they attempt to sneak into the school an hour before the morning bell on Mondays to get a preview of the new words.

In Section Five, the focus is on using facts, history, research, self-analysis, and a little espionage to get students to think analytically and write informatively. By emphasizing the many heroes, inventors, and achievers of African American descent who are not found in many textbooks, Tracie Pullum describes a lesson plan that merges research, history, and art with writing.

Section Six looks at creative writing, an area in which teachers seem to either flourish or fear to tread. For Bohemian teachers like Greg Stanley, however, creative writing holds delightful possibilities. Stanley describes an outrageous exercise in creativity in which he asks students to rewrite well-known American writings in the styles of equally famous American writers. In his activity, he requests that his students rewrite "The Pledge of Allegiance" in the style of Edgar Allan Poe's poem "The Bells."

Even the best student writers often have difficulty grasping the more subtle aspects of writing, such as tone and point of view. In Section Seven, the activities involve communicating feelings through innuendo, understanding perspectives from "Someone Else's Shoes," and helping students develop an appreciation for nuance. Although many of the activities in *Going Bohemian* involve literature in some way, the activities in Section Eight operate off of specific works or attempt to teach particular literary devices. Mike Rychlik describes how his students use characters and events from recently read novels as fodder for the writing of poetry.

Section Nine advocates having fun with rhyming, riddles, and research. Clarissa West-White describes an intriguing activity that uses research that students gather through self-selected topics as the catalyst for the creation of an autobiographical poem.

In all, *Going Bohemian* offers teachers the good stuff without much filler—45 activities that can be taught over approximately 100 days of schooling. Perhaps the most impressive aspect about the book is that the activities work well with students of all backgrounds and levels, as is evidenced in the student samples provided. When I recently used "Performance Art Poetry" (an activity from the Multimedia section) with a class of high school juniors, the lesson took place over the course of 2 weeks. Every day, students wrote, pondered, discussed, pored over dictionaries and thesauruses, rewrote, rewrote again, and then practiced presenting their multimedia poems to the class. Rather than the usual complaints about workload or the drudgery of composition, students became totally immersed in the activity at hand. After 2 weeks of intensive writing, instead of planning a mutiny, they asked if they could do it again.

Unquestionably, teaching students to write well is difficult, often vexing work. But literacy lasts a lifetime. A teacher might react to the challenge of teaching writing by retreating to the safe obscurity of theoretical frameworks or by kowtowing to the fluctuating whims of the state. Or a teacher could decide to chuck the bureaucracy, address the needs of the human beings in the classroom, and "go Bohemian." *Going Bohemian* is about adopting high standards, an artistic sensibility, and a unshakable belief in the power of words.

Lawrence Baines and Anthony Kunkel

On Assessment

IT WAS EARLY ON IN MY FIRST YEAR OF TEACHING that I realized how little I knew about the assessment of student writing. After a rough beginning, I had finally begun to transform my class into a writing environment. As the students became more receptive to writing, their papers began increasing in length, and particularly, in tone.

There was a young boy, who I had been told was learning disabled, in one of my classes. This boy had an imagination that astounded me. I encouraged him to write; I told him to abandon caution and let his soul spill onto the paper. And he did. He brought me a several-page story one day, and I could tell by how nervous he was that he had written something special. I took the papers from his hands, but he stood there for a moment not knowing what to do with them, holding them still, as if the memory of the papers in his fingers gave him comfort. I read his story. He had invented a superhero who was at battle with an evil force that lived within himself. It was truly a beautiful story, yet he had misspelled more than half the words. There were commas in random places and sentences that ran together with no thought for pauses or phrasing, and the words *and, or, so,* and *then* repeated again and again. Yet he stood in front of me wanting to know what I thought of his story. This boy was the superhero. Without realizing it, he had written his own story. I told him that it was beyond good. I told him that it was one of the best stories I had ever read from a student. And it was. Based on my objectives and expectations, I gave him an "A."

There was a quiet 14-year-old girl in one of my morning classes who never smiled, even though she always did everything I asked and did it very well. My class had been writing rough drafts for reflective essays, and I had requested that they reflect on a memory that carried some powerful emotions. On the second day of writing I noticed the tears falling onto this young girl's paper. When I moved closer to her, she leaned over her paper, but continued to write. I knelt beside her and asked her quietly if she would consider writing about something less painful. She shook her head faintly, almost imperceptibly, and continued writing.

On the third day of writing the reflective essays, the students were put into groups for peer critiques. As I handed out my guidelines, the girl informed me that she did not want to let anyone read her essay. I felt that it might do her some good to get the feedback of others, so I told her not to be shy and that she should get used to letting others critique her work. For a moment she sat there shaking her head, then she abruptly grabbed her paper and walked out of class. Stunned, I quickly followed after her. She was standing there crying, and without a word she handed me her crumpled essay. I began reading her story. It was beautiful.

She described the ride from her mom's house to her uncle's with all the wonder and excitement of an 8-year-old child. The imagery was vivid; she wrote that the sun woke up the flowers that lined her uncle's driveway and she described the fragrance of jasmine through the senses of a child. She was saddened to bid farewell to her mother. I was shocked to read the description of her torment and confusion as her uncle viciously raped her for the first time. Although her story was terrifying, her writing was lovely. She used long compound sentences for description, followed by short powerful sentences for effect. As I walked her to the guidance counselor's office, I wondered how I would put a grade on a paper like this. I never did, but in my grade book I put an "A."

When students write they are only equal in that they are individuals. Writing is individual. Assessment, therefore, needs to be individual as well. Just as the student who has to struggle for every word in every sentence deserves one grade, the gifted writer who makes no effort to write beyond the simplest expectations deserves another. If assessing writing were a sure thing, there would be a great deal more writing within in the English classrooms. The reality of a typical classroom today is diversity, and given the nature of this diversity, the writing teacher has to create the rubric of expectations. It is not likely that a standard five-paragraph essay will require the same criteria as a prose passage that calls for images to be used as central metaphors. It is up to the teacher to decide exactly what is expected with each piece.

Assessment has been researched extensively, and perhaps the most comprehensive information available will point a person toward holistic evaluation. However, the teacher who chooses to really make his or her students write ultimately must find a comfort zone that allows for teacher feedback as well as assessment.

For the teacher who encourages his or her 120 to 180 students to write 15 to 20 pages a week, it could be assumed that there will be an abundance of assessment needed, but this is not necessarily so. Does it make sense to have students write less so that all work may be graded or commented on? If they are writing more and I am still providing as much, if not more, feedback than if they were writing less, does it matter if I have not read every word they have written?

I believe it is the writing that counts, not the amount of reading I do. I have heard other English teachers state that they read every word their students write. I could spend countless hours attempting to read everything I have my students write, but that would become frustrating, and I would more than likely ask them to write less. I have a standard policy in my classes: *Everything that is written is subject to a grade, but not everything written will receive one.* I use an abundance of "skill building" activities in class, and during these I work with the students, answering questions and providing feedback as they write. Usually I follow such activities with a major assignment that puts the new skills into practice. These assignments usually have no length requirements, but I ask the students to limit their writing to under 20 pages, unless they feel that is impossible. At the beginning of the year, there is always apprehension, but it does not take long for even the most reluctant of writers to realize that some pieces do require some extensive development.

On longer assignments, I generally have a rubric in mind (or written out) of my expectations, and I provide the students with these expectations at the onset of the assignment. When grading, I make a point to mark only on the first three pages and then focus in as a holistic reader. Because most assignments are worked on extensively during class, I am familiar with specific problems each writer has had and questions they have asked. Individuality and effort always count.

For many assignments, I incorporate oral presentations into the grading. Oral presentations are a useful vehicle for students to share work with peers, and they allow the teacher to provide instant feedback. I have found that by not forcing the students to read their work aloud, more often than not, they are more receptive to do so.

To address the worry of some students that I may have overlooked some of their better work, I also incorporate a portfolio into my grading. Each grading term, which is 9 weeks in my school, I require the students to put together selected pieces that they are particularly proud of, especially work that was done in class but not recognized. This works well in two ways: First it lets students know that their best work can be counted as a grade, even if it was not one of the graded assignments, and second, it allows me an opportunity to pick and choose what I wish to grade without worrying that I will have missed a significant piece of writing by any of my students.

However you choose to assess students' work, it is important to reconsider the stigmatic tradition of grading everything that is ever written in class. Students today more than ever need to write. Moving past the simplicity of "process writing" and teaching students to write instinctively will enhance both the quality of their writing and also the quality of their discovery. Once a student experiences hearing his or her own writer's voice, he or she will find it frustrating to accept anything less than quality. Writing at this point becomes very personal.

Anthony Kunkel

From a Student

A FORMER TEACHER OF MINE RECENTLY ASKED me to write about what I experience on a typical day in the classroom. I thought about this for some time and decided that I'd like to give you a tangible sense of how students see the classroom and the teachers running those classes. This is an image from the flip side. The faces peering from behind the desk are more than just scenery.

Fourth Period

I walk into class, my mind buzzing with the social static I picked up in the halls. I hail some friends and slide into my seat, ready to make my grade for the day. The teacher rises languidly from his desk and stands to face the class. He gazes at us tiredly for a moment, then moves to the board to write our assignment for the day: Page 290 (1–7), 297 (1–12). Book work again—oh boy. The teacher returns to his seat and begins scratching at some papers with a stubby red pencil. Some of the students open their books, but most begin in friendly conversation. Quickly the conversation turns to loud talking, then progresses to some yells and laughing. The teacher slams his pencil down and jumps from his desk like a jack-in-the-box. "Be quiet and do the assignment or I'm gonna start writing people up!" he shouts while waving a pink slip at us, the same one he's waved all year. The class becomes quiet, paying lip service to his authority, and a few more students open their books.

I look up one answer after another. Henry V, Battle of Hastings, Industrial Revolution—these are just names, words. That's all the book asks for. I copy a passage, rewrite a sentence, and look for a key word or phrase, one after another. I find it in the book and write it on paper. The only thing I know about the Battle of Hastings is that it's the answer to number 5. Occasionally I don't answer a question completely. No big deal; I doubt he'll read it anyway.

When I finish, I walk up to the teacher's desk and lay the paper on the small stack that has already been finished. His head never lifts, and his pencil continues to slash red across words and numbers. Some in the class read faster than I do and are already finished. They have moved to the back of the class and pulled out the cards—rummy today, or spades. I glance at the clock; we have 20 minutes left. Most students haven't finished yet, and some haven't even begun. They are waiting for a friend to finish so they can copy their answers. They aren't really cheating, just increasing the efficiency of their writing. They'll learn the same whether they copy from a book or from a friend. I lay my head down and sleep. Soon the bell rings, and I leave class knowing nothing more about Henry V than I did when I walked in—except that he's the answer to number 3.

Fifth Period

I take my seat, journal ready, and wait for the bell. A few stragglers slide in just before the bell and grab their journals from the box, then move straight to their seats. The teacher stands at his podium in front of the class, watching as the desks fill. When the bell rings we speak quietly as he takes roll. One brave soul slips over to a neighboring table and the teacher pauses and asks, "Michael, what are you doing?" Michael shakes his head embarrassed and skitters back to his desk. The teacher finishes taking roll then greets the class. Most have their journals open with a pen or pencil ready. "Alright, everyone, you know the deal. Let's spend about 10 minutes on the journals, then we'll move on."

The class quietly bends to the task. This is always one of my favorite parts. We write, sometimes on a topic, sometimes not. There is no sound but pencils moving. The room is like a cathedral. No one talks and no one stops writing. To speak during journals would be akin to heresy. When the teacher finally breaks the silence with a single "OK," there is a palpable sigh, and subdued voices start up again, still low, but now permissible. It doesn't take long, however, for the students' attention to become focused on the man standing in front of the class. My neighbor and I exchange a few words, but are quickly caught in a wave of "shush" that comes from our classmates.

The teacher has us wrapped around his finger, and he knows it. He stares at the class for a moment, looking from face to face, then smiles. "Today we are going to begin writing screenplays," he says.

Yesterday it was commercials. Last week, we studied and created metaphors. Everyday it's something new. The class waits, anticipating, wondering how, knowing he'll tell us. Everyone gets involved; you cannot slip by in this class, and we all know it. Even those who come to school just to get out of the house participate.

I watch him in front of the class, describing narrative styles as if he's preaching the Gospel, and look around at the class. Everyone is watching the overhead projector, watching his writing flow across the screen, making it look simple. It never is, though. He makes sure of it. This class is for thinking. He's not a stickler for spelling or grammar; it's all about creation.

Today's screenplays are just one plank of a bridge that he's teaching us to build. As he nears the end of his instructions, the class becomes jittery. We know that shortly he'll set us free to run with the ideas he's inspired. It's like he's turned on the tap and our ideas have begun to flow. Each of us begins to create. The class begins discussing ideas for their screenplays. Our small groups within the class have become competitive with the other groups, and we all wish to outdo each other. The teacher wanders from group to group, jumping into conversations and bouncing ideas off of us, sometimes so hard it hurts. The hush in the class disappears, replaced by the buzz of creation.

No one I know can inspire this amount of zeal into my normally sluggish classmates. He has plowed our minds through careful practice of each skill, each technique, and each mindset necessary to write the way he expects us to. And we *want* to write as well as he expects us to. We've learned point-of-view writing, mood writing, description, and persuasion. We've practiced writing everything from short stories to radio jingles, from poems to magazine ads, but at this moment knowledge steps aside and ability begins to take over; he is teaching us instincts. We can feel a good sentence, use metaphors without noticing, and know immediately when a piece of writing needs a revision. The difference between good and bad writing, independent from any rules or guidelines, has become clear.

I pause in mid-paragraph to consider a phrase, rework it in my mind, knowing I can make it better, and the bell rings. I look at the clock for the first time since class has started. It seems as if we have just begun. As I put my work away and begin preparing for my next class, I'm still reworking the phrase in my mind.

Rob Jones
11th Grade
Dixie County High School
Cross City, Florida, USA

Anything is a structure. If we presuppose that some things are structures and other things are substantive elements which go into structures, we have trapped ourselves at the outset. Everything is both, which is to say that things and relations are matters of conceptual option. To understand the option one is playing one must be aware of where one has mentally placed himself.

Moffet, J. (1983). *Teaching the universe of discourse* (p. 2). Boston, MA: Houghton Mifflin.

STARTING OUT

"EXACTLY WHAT IS YOUR THEORETICAL FRAMEWORK? As a teacher, you must be well-grounded in a theoretical framework or you simply will not be able to function effectively in the classroom."

The words of the professor in your graduate class ring in your ears as you drive home in the dark. You think to yourself: Theoretical framework? When was the last time that prof was in a real classroom?

Perhaps it was insane to sign up for a graduate class at night while you held down a full-time teaching position at a secondary school almost 20 miles away. You had just finished the first week of school, and it had been the usual chaos of textbook distribution, seating charts, over-crowded classrooms, and endless faculty meetings after school. Your fingers were inkstained in red, your hair was beyond hope, and the odor of sweaty, hormone-crazy adolescents seemed to follow you wherever you went.

As you think about your school day, it seems that you barely had enough time for a bathroom break, let alone time to reflect on the extent to which you are a facilitative, student-centered, em-powering, inclusive teacher. Besides having to read six sets of writing samples over the weekend, you are in the process of moving into a new apartment, you must work on getting a billing problem settled with your Internet provider, and you have to buy your mother a gift for her birthday next week. One thing is for certain: This weekend you won't have time to sit around, pontificate, and go through the academic exercise of lining up some esoteric sound-ing, fictitious theoretical framework. You'll think up something scholarly to pacify the professor later. For Monday, you want to teach an activity that will get students' attention and give you a chance to see how well they are able to think and write. You have no time to waste. You've decided to go Bohemian.

Activity	Entry point	Students work on	Preparation time needed
Adagio	Music, film clip	Descriptive writing	Substantial (with film clip), minimal (with only music)
J to the 3rd Power	Journals	Expressive writing	Minimal
Thermometer Reading	Graphic representation	Reflective writing	Substantial (need copies of handout and samples)
Modeling Prose	Contemporary literature	Style	Substantial (need copies of handout and pos-sibly some books)
120-Word Sentence	Passage from Faulkner	Creating long sentences	Minimal

Lawrence Baines

Adagio

Type of activity: Individual. Approximate time: One class period.

Objective

Students will learn to attach images and words to music.

Materials

Recording of Samuel Barber's "Adagio for Strings," compact disc or cassette player, drawing paper, pens, and crayons.

Set-Up

Tell students that you are going to play a piece of music and that you want them to write down four to seven images that the music evokes in their minds. In addition, ask that students create one drawing. The drawing need not be artistically brilliant or realistic, but should accurately reflect the nature of the music. Especially encourage students to use colors.

Procedure

After the song, give students 15 minutes to finish writing. They may want to put their thoughts into a poem, a story, or simply work further on their drawing.

Have students show their works of art and read their text to the class. It usually works best if students explain their drawings first, then read what they wrote. Repeat any particularly effective phrase or astute description.

After several students have shown their work, try to summarize and synthesize students' comments.

Summary

Through music, image, and word, Adagio often enables students who are usually not particularly gifted writers to create a solid piece of writing.

Enrichment

After students have revised and completed their work, play the first few minutes of the movie *Platoon* (directed by Oliver Stone), which uses Barber's "Adagio for Strings" as part of its soundtrack. Inevitably, a student will have drawn or written about one of the images that Stone devised for the screen.

ADAGIO STUDENT SAMPLE

- grassy meadows in the rain
- death of a lover (the other crying)
- emotional goodbye between 2 friends
- falling off a building in slow motion
- soldiers slowly marching to war

The inside symbol is a Hindu sign for life or sustaining life. I don't know where the outside of the circle came from — but it kinda looks like feet marching...

Pamela Sissi Carroll

Journal to the Third Power

**Type of activity:
Individual journal writing.
Approximate time: 45 minutes.**

Preamble

Are you convinced that there is some value in having your students write journals, but disillusioned with the aimless entries students produce during their 5- or 10-minute freewriting sessions? The Triple-Entry Journal, which my students refer to as the Journal to the Third Power, or simply the "J3," may be a solution. Simply stated, the J3 is a type of journal that encourages students to think about their reactions to any of the stimuli that are important to our lessons, including group work sessions, literary texts, grammar and mechanics, plays and dramatizations, television shows and movies, advertisements, works of visual and performing art, guest speakers, and World Wide Web sites. In the description that follows, I will refer to each of these with the words *text* or *texts* in order to avoid clumsiness; however, I do not intend to suggest that the J3 is valuable only when used with a printed text.

So What is the J3, Exactly?

The J3 is based on these simple premises:

1. Students enjoy expressing their own opinions about the texts with which they come into contact, in and beyond our classrooms.

2. Students benefit as thinkers when we offer them the opportunity to make sense of texts for themselves.

3. Students can use journals to explore their own thinking. Through writing journal entries, students are given space to play with ideas—to articulate initial responses then follow the ideas to see where they lead. In J3 entries, students can begin going in one direction, then change course and continue; they can argue with themselves, uncover gaps in their own understandings, and discover what it is that they really want to say about texts.

4. Students who take the time to write journal entries deserve to have responses made to those entries; through responses to their work, students begin to see themselves as writers.

5. Education, including learning to write, is a social activity; students need the opportunity to interact with peers and with adults as they grow academically and socially.

The J3 is a format that students can easily learn to use when they write in their journals and when they respond to peers' journal entries. I have found that students like to be given the choice of using one of two J3 designs.

Some students will prefer to use an inverted T design, in which the page is split down the middle with a vertical line that begins at the top of the page and ends two thirds of the way to the bottom of the page. A horizontal line is added to separate the columns from the bottom one third of the page. The two columns are for the writer, and the space at the bottom is for the responder.

Other students will prefer to use a block design. For this design, two thick horizontal lines are made across the page to create three blocks of space that are approximately the same size. The two thirds at the top of the page, like the columns in the inverted T format, is for the original writer; the bottom one third is for the responder.

Objective

WHAT MAKES THIS FORMAT/STRATEGY DIFFERENT FROM FREEWRITING JOURNALS?

The J3 encourages focused freewriting. Students are given the freedom to decide which aspects of the text are meaningful to them, and therefore they are encouraged to make sense of the text for themselves instead of waiting for someone else to tell them what it means. Nevertheless, it does provide some structure, direction, and purpose; students react to specific features of the text first, then examine their reactions. This sequence moves students into critical thinking more readily than does the journal format in which they write initial reactions to a text then move on to another assignment. In the latter case, students may never consider how a text evoked satisfaction, confusion, dissatisfaction, and other strong feelings. By using the J3 format and thinking strategy, students first capture initial responses then explore them.

The J3 allows students to receive responses to their ideas shortly after the ideas are written down. In traditional classrooms, teachers are not able to read and write comments on students' every time they ask students to write entries. Students need occasions in which they write for readers who are not teachers; the J3 allows them this opportunity.

Students' entries in the first column give their teachers clues about the words and phrases that the students are using to make sense of reading passages, class discussions, group projects, guest speakers' talks, and other daily happenings. Students' entries in the second column help teachers understand the students' thought processes.

Materials

Paper and pen.

Set-Up and Procedure

HOW DO STUDENTS CREATE A J3?

To begin J3 entries, writer-thinkers write down specific parts of the text that catch their attention, including specific written or spoken passages or phrases, individual words, facts, paraphrases, movements, colors, or shapes. This part of the entry is written in the left-hand column (or the top one third) of the page. Page numbers and other appropriate citations should be added in this part of the students' entries. If practical, writer-thinkers can experiment with the effect of leaving their initial entries alone for a few hours. They are likely to find, when they return to their writing, that they can read their own entries from the stance of readers instead of as writers if there has been a lapse of time between the acts of composing and reviewing their initial entries.

Second, students will write about the words, phrases, and questions that they have written in part one of their J3. This part of the entry is written in the right-hand column (or middle section) of the page. Here, they will explain or describe their reactions to these aspects or write questions that were raised in their minds because of the phrases, words, and facts that are identified. In essence, the writer-thinkers are talking to themselves about why the passages they selected during the first step caught their attention.

Third, the students exchange their J3 entries with peers. Reader-responders read the initial and second entries, then write responses to the writer-thinker. A conversation is thus begun in written form; this conversation focuses on the writer-thinkers' reactions to the text and the reader-responders' comments on those reactions.

Ideally, teachers will allow students a few minutes following quiet writing, reading, and responding time for oral conversations in which the reader-responders and writer-thinkers expound on their written comments. Note that each student will finish the J3 activity having filled two roles: writer-thinker and reader-responder.

Summary

WHAT ARE SOME OF THE PROBLEMS I COULD EXPERIENCE IF I IMPLEMENT THE J3 STRATEGY?

1. Students must be given enough time to work as both writer-thinkers and reader-responders. For teachers who like to use the first or final 5 minutes for journal writing, this increased time demand may be a problem.

2. Students' ideas, not the teacher's, will receive top billing and will provide the direction for discussions related to the topics written about in students' J3 entries. Teachers who are uncomfortable sharing with students the responsibility for determining the direction of class discussions may find that this shift of responsibility is a problem for them. Sometimes teachers feel guilty of neglecting their responsibility if they are not telling students what to think about literary texts and other curricular materials; for those teachers, this approach may be disconcerting.

3. Traditional grading schemes are inappropriate for this kind of journal, because a collaborative effort is required for each complete entry.

Teachers will have to develop alternative ways of assessing the quality of students' work in their J3 journals.

I suggest the use of a grading rubric that is designed specifically and used exclusively with the J3. My students have helped me develop a system in which I mark their pages with these labels:

ETP ("Extremely thought provoking!")

MMST ("Made me stop and think!")

TATMK ("Think about this more, kiddo!")

WTE ("Where's the effort?")

After several weeks, students quit trying to translate these marks into letter grades and began working toward eliciting positive responses to their work rather than writing only for a grade.

Enrichment

I like to ask students when they are in the reader-responder role to circle the words of the writer-thinker that stand out most vividly to them. When the partners talk about their journals, the circled words become a focal point. The reader-responder may discuss why he or she marked them, or may ask questions about them. The circled portion then becomes the place that the writer-thinker begins with a new piece of writing. The writer-thinker may compose an essay that begins by centering attention on the circled words, write a poem or design a word puzzle that includes them, or try other creative extensions. In this extension, "looping" is an added feature. The journal becomes a source that generates ideas for another piece of writing, and the second piece of writing responds to a reader's comments.

Tom Stewart

Thermometer Reading

Type of activity: Individual (prewriting).
Approximate time: One class period.

Objective

Students will understand the relevance of their own lives as a source for an abundance of writing topics.

Materials

Preprinted thermometer handouts (preferably on colored paper) and an overhead projector. (See page 12 for the handout.)

Set-Up

Conduct a brief class discussion about how temperature fluctuates from positives to negatives, as do the events that make up our own lives.

Procedure

Using the preprinted thermometer, model an example of what is expected with the overhead projector. Ten positive (good) events will be listed beside the numbers *above* the zero degree mark, and 10 negative (bad) events will be listed beside the numbers *below* the zero degree mark. These events should be listed from best to worst, and read aloud to the class. Students should then, with little guidance, be able to complete their own thermometers by following the model provided. Based on the age and skill level of the class, the number of events should be adjusted appropriately. Once all students have completed their thermometer, ideas will have blossomed and topics for personal essays will be available.

Summary

This lesson is the way I begin my school year. Personal reflection and writing seem easiest for students to grasp, and it gives them a confidence boost necessary to tackle more complicated forms. The thermometer activity, besides being a good way to get to know your students, will hopefully solve any problems you might have with students who might tell you "I don't know what to write about."

Note: It is a good idea to publish the thermometers somewhere around the classroom, but use caution. Some of the students will include very personal and painful details of their lives and will not want them published in view of their peers.

Enrichment

Each student should select a single event from his or her thermometer and use this as the subject for a personal narrative.

Use this unit in collaboration with a science teacher who teaches how temperature affects the mercury in a thermometer. Students might want to consider how seasonal fluctuations affect their creative processes. Do they feel more creative when it is cold and snowy or bright and sunny?

THERMOMETER READING HANDOUT

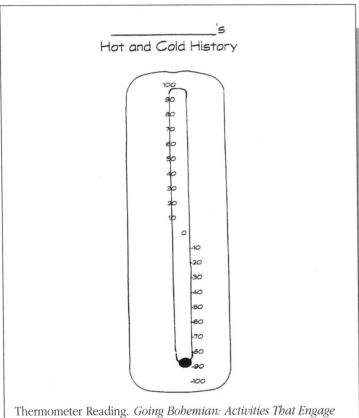

_____'s
Hot and Cold History

Thermometer Reading. *Going Bohemian: Activities That Engage Adolescents in the Art of Writing Well* by Lawrence Baines and Anthony Kunkel. Copyright 1999 by the International Reading Association. May be copied for classroom use only.

THERMOMETER READING STUDENT SAMPLE

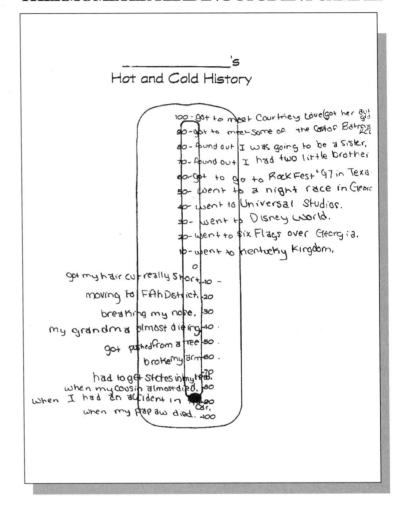

_____'s
Hot and Cold History

100 - got to meet Courtney Love (got her autograph)
90 - got to meet some of the cast of Batman
80 - found out I was going to be a sister,
70 - found out I had two little brothers
60 - got to go to RockFest '97 in Texas
50 - went to a night race in Georgia
40 - went to Universal Studios.
30 - went to Disney World.
20 - went to Six Flags over Georgia.
10 - went to Kentucky Kingdom,

got my hair cut really short -10 -
moving to Fifth District. -20
breaking my nose. -30
My grandma almost dieing -40 -
got pushed from a tree -50 -
broke my arm -60 .
had to get stitches in my head. -70.
when my cousin almost died. -80
When I had an accident in the car, -90
when my Papaw died. -100

Lawrence Baines

Modeling Prose

Type of activity: Individual.
Approximate time: 50 minutes.

Objective

Students will learn how to write in three distinctly different styles—those of authors John Grisham, Sue Grafton, and Thomas Pynchon. Modeling Prose also shows students how to make their writing more interesting. Teachers who find the prose of Grisham, Grafton, and Pynchon too commercial may want to choose excerpts from *Cannery Row* by John Steinbeck, *Holiday Memory* by Dylan Thomas, and *In Another Country* by Ernest Hemingway.

Materials

You'll need to be able to read aloud from the literature you select and have copies of prose excerpts to hand out to students before beginning the assignment. The Distinctive Style handout on the following page includes excerpts from the works of Grisham, Grafton, and Pynchon.

Set-Up

Tell students that they are going to learn different ways to express themselves using three distinctive styles. Read two or three pages aloud from each work.

Procedure

Hand out a copy of the Distinctive Style worksheet. Ask students to read the three excerpts silently, then ask a student to read each excerpt aloud. Instruct students to write three pieces—one each in the style they have been presented. The exercise works best if students write on a similar theme as the excerpt, attempt to remain true to the style, yet use autobiographical information.

Finally, share student responses, and have the class vote on the best representation of each style.

Summary

Sometimes only by adapting the writing style of a different author can students learn to appreciate the highly individualistic nature of writing. After participating in Modeling Prose once or twice, many students will begin to borrow aspects of other writers' styles and will learn to adapt them to serve their own needs. By having students model prose occasionally, a student's range of expression can be enhanced greatly.

Enrichment

Modeling Prose is a great exercise from which to jump to style, tone, or comparison and contrast essays.

MODELING PROSE HANDOUT

DISTINCTIVE STYLE

1. Substitute your relationship with one of your parents or siblings, change the nature of the relationship and your career. Keep first person point of view.

   From Grisham, J. (1997). *The Rainmaker* (p. 1). New York: Doubleday.

   My decision to become a lawyer was irrevocably sealed when I realized my father hated the legal profession. I was a young teenager, clumsy, embarrassed by my awkwardness, frustrated with life, horrified of puberty, about to be shipped off to a military school by my father for insubordination. He was an ex-Marine who believed boys should live by the crack of the whip. I'd developed a quick tongue and an aversion to discipline, and his solution was simply to send me away. It was years before I forgave him.

   He was also an industrial engineer who worked seventy hours a week for a company that made, among many other items, ladders. Because by their nature ladders are dangerous devices, his company became a frequent target of lawsuits. And because he handled design, my father was the favorite choice to speak for the company in depositions and trials. I can't say that I blame him for hating lawyers, but I grew to admire them because they made his life so miserable. He'd spend eight hours haggling with them, then hit the martinis as soon as he walked in the door. No hellos. No hugs. No dinner.

2. Select a day other than January 8 and use something other than running as your outlet. Keep first person point of view.

   From Grafton, S. (1997). *M Is for Malice* (p. 1). New York: Henry Holt & Company.

   Robert Deitz came back into my life on Wednesday, January 8. I remember the date because it was Elvis Presley's birthday and one of the local radio stations had announced it would spend the next twenty-four hours playing every song he'd ever sung. At six a.m. my clock radio blared on, playing "Heartbreak Hotel" at top volume. I smacked the Off button with the flat of my hand and rolled out of bed as usual. I pulled on my sweats in preparation for my morning run. I brushed my teeth, splashed water on my face, and trotted down the spiral stairs. I locked my front door behind me, moved out to the street where I did an obligatory stretch, leaning against the gatepost in front of my apartment. The day was destined to be a strange one, involving as it did a dreaded lunch date with Tasha Howard, one of my recently discovered first cousins. Running was the only way I could think of to quell my uneasiness. I headed for the bike path that parallels the beach.

   (continued)

MODELING PROSE HANDOUT (continued)

DISTINCTIVE STYLE

3. Change the year and the city. Maintain the third person perspective.
   From Pynchon, T. (1997). *Mason & Dixie* (p. 6). New York: Henry Holt & Company.

   This Christmastide of 1786, with the War settl'd and the Nation bickering itself into Fragments, wounds bodily and ghostly, great and small, go aching on, not ev'ry one commemorated,—nor, too often, even re-counted. Snow lies upon all Philadelphia, from River to River, whose further shores have so vanish'd behind curtains of ice-fog that the City today might be an Isle upon an Ocean. Ponds and Creeks are frozen over, and the Trees a-glare to the last slightest Twig,—Nerve-Lines of concentrated Light. Hammers and Saws have fallen still, bricks lie in snowcover'd heaps, City-Sparrow, in speckled' Outbursts, hop in and out of what Shelter there may be,—the nightward Sky, Clouds blown to Chalksmears, stretches above the Northern Liberties, Spring Garden and Germantown, its early moon pale as the Snow-Drifts,—smoke ascends from Chimney-Pots, Sledging-Parties adjourn indoors, Taverns bustle,—freshly infus'd Coffee flows ev'ryplace, borne about thro' Rooms front and back, whilst Madeira, which as ever fuel'd Association in these Parts, is deploy'd nowadays like an ancient Elixir upon the seething Pot of Politics,—for the Times are as impossible to calculate, this Advent, as the Distance to a star.

Lawrence Baines

120-Word Sentence

**Type of activity: Individual.
Approximate time: 20 minutes.**

Objective

Students will use clauses and phrases appropriately to create a legitimate, eloquent, very long sentence.

Materials

Pen and paper or a computer with a word-processing program.

Set-Up

Read a few long sentences by famous authors. One of my favorites is a passage from "A Rose for Emily" by William Faulkner.

> They held the funeral on the second day, with the town coming to look at Miss Emily beneath a mass of bought flowers, with the crayon face of her father musing profoundly above the bier and the ladies sibilant and macabre; and the very old men—some in their brushed Confederate uniforms—on the porch and the lawn, talking of Miss Emily as if she had been a contemporary of theirs, believing that they had danced with her and courted her perhaps, confusing time with its mathematical progression, as the old do, to whom all the past is not a diminishing road but, instead, a huge meadow which no winter ever quite touches, divided from them now by the narrow bottle-neck of the most recent decade of years. (128 words)
>
> (Faulkner, W. (1987). A rose for Emily. In L. Fowler, G. Walker, & K. McCormick (Eds.), *The Lexington introduction to literature* (p. 258). Lexington, KY: D.C. Heath & Company.)

Discuss Faulkner's technique. Highlight prepositions (*beneath, with, of, above*) and how he uses a variety of phrases.

Write a very long sentence as a class. Pick a topic such as "Let's write a sentence about trying to sort out what's important in life." Solicit suggestions from the class and write them on the board or transparency so they can see how clauses and phrases can be used to elaborate and extend an idea.

Procedure

Tell students to write two 120-word sentences. The exercise works best if students write about whatever is on their minds at the moment: a forthcoming athletic contest, a date, a personal problem, or an exam next period.

After they have written one or two sentences, have students read them aloud. When they are finished, ask students to identify the specific techniques they used to elongate the sentence, including the phrases, gerunds, conjunctions, and other devices.

Summary

The 120-Word Sentence is a great exercise to use when your students' writing seems overly reliant on dull subject-verb-noun structures. The 120-Word Sentence also helps alert students to the possibility of sentence rhythm. For example, later in the same story, Faulkner writes the following sentence as a single paragraph: "The man himself lay in the bed."

Enrichment

A nice follow-up to the 120-Word Sentence is to have students alter sentence structure again. Have students trade papers and rewrite their single 120-word sentence into at least seven different sentences.

In a society that demands its work force have an increasingly sophisticated knowledge of computers and technology, access to and use of computers during elementary and secondary education can provide students with an important knowledge base that can increase their opportunities for employment and success in the job market.

National Center for Education Statistics. (1998). *The Condition of Education 1998.* [Online]. Washington, DC: U.S. Government Printing Office. Available: http://nces.ed.gov/pubs98/condition98/c98seca.html

MULTIMEDIA

YOU ARE NOT AFRAID OF USING TECHNOLOGY, EXACTLY. Although it may be true that you've never been able to program your video-cassette recorder, you think you could learn how to do it if you thought this might be of benefit.

But you like film, you have surfed the Internet a little, and you acknowledge that multimedia has the potential to bring a topic to life in ways that a pure lecture and discussion format never could. Today's students are bombarded with media messages—radio, the Internet, music, computer games, advertising, cable channels, e-mail, digital video disc, video—and you are not sure whether you should offer your classroom as a sanctuary against these forces or as a research center for their analysis and evaluation.

Being a Bohemian, you cannot deny the power of the art that is emerging from the electronic media or the influence of the media on your students' perceptions of truth and reality. So you begin to experiment with multimedia—not as a gimmick to wow students momentarily, but as a tool through which you can effectively improve students' facilities with reading, writing, and speaking.

The world is changing. In order to keep the written word alive—in order to keep literature, language, and composition relevant—you must reformulate some of your lessons so that they engage students where they are, deep in the vortex of electronic media, and take them to vistas you want them to know—the undiscovered country of words, reflection, and ideas.

Once you begin the trek, there is no turning back. Your students will respond enthusiastically when you integrate multimedia, and you will continually search for ways to link multimedia experiences to works of great literature. For you know that great literature only remains viable if it speaks to the lives of readers today.

Activity	Entry point	Students work on	Preparation time needed
Pop-Up Videos	VH1	Research, grammar, and punctuation	Substantial
Sudden Performance	Short short stories	Reading and oral interpretation	Minimal
Online Writing for an E-Zine	Online e-zines	Collaborative fiction writing	Substantial
Spin Doctors and Truth	Television news, newspapers, radio programs	Critical analysis, fact and opinion, objectivity and subjectivity	Substantial
Performance Art Poetry	Scripted poem	Word choice, aesthetics	Minimal (during initial stages), substantial (with the integration of PowerPoint)

Leslie Atwater

Pop-Up Videos

Type of activity: Cooperative groups of two to four students. Approximate time: Five 50-minute periods.

Objective

Students will use research skills to uncover facts, analyze and understand contemporary lyrics, dramatically interpret a song, and use appropriate punctuation and grammar.

Materials

Media center access, cassette player and/or CD player, video cassette, VCR, white poster board, and markers. Availability of computers with Internet access is also useful.

Set-Up

Videotape a small clip of the show *Pop-Up Videos* (these are music videos that contain spontaneous pop-up blurbs of random research and information) from the VH1 cable channel, and reserve the media center (or access to) for 2 days of classes. A tripod and VCR with television will also need to be reserved. Enough poster board or white poster paper for student use will be needed. Students will be required to select a song that is appropriate for the classroom and to supply that song on CD or cassette, along with the written-out lyrics of that song.

Procedure

Have students view the recorded sample of *Pop-Up Videos*, and instruct them that they will be creating a video of their own that will also require them to do some research. Spend the next 2 days in the media center familiarizing students with resources available for doing research and allowing students to begin their research projects. Assign each student the task of discovering five different facts:

Facts that relate to the musicians

Facts that relate to the subject of the song

Information relating to a song lyric

Details relating to one of the musical instruments played by the performer

One fact that all members of the research group have in common

In addition, each of these five facts must have at least three supporting or elaborating sentences.

On the fourth day of the lesson, students should choose their three favorite researched facts and transfer each fact to an individual piece of white poster board. Students will use these poster boards as pop-ups as they plan and rehearse a skit and a musical theme for their own "music video" by holding them up at the appropriate places during the playing of the music. The last day of the project should involve videotaping student skits that are accompanied by the song students have researched.

Summary

Creating pop-up videos is a refreshing and exhilarating experience. When we did this activity in class, the amount of enthusiasm students expressed was amazing not only to me but to all the teachers on my team. Allowing students to combine research with a song they enjoy seems to stimulate them and give them incentive to create something artistic. Through every step of the project, students discussed, laughed, and researched intensely. The resulting videos of student skits have been remarkable.

Enrichment

A painless way to get students to write a comparison-contrast essay is to ask them to compare the recording that they chose for their pop-up video to other music videos by the same artist.

POP-UP VIDEO STUDENT WORKSHEET SAMPLE

Name_____

Group #_____

Performance Date:_____

Song - Walkin on the Sun
by Smash Mouth

Pop-Up Videos

Directions: As a group, you will perform a song while holding up nonfiction facts that you have researched in the library. You are individually required to research the following five subjects and then choose your favorite three to transfer onto poster board. Every group member must have different information. On Friday your groups facts will be held up as your group presents a skit for a music video.

When researching the below topics, you must write a minimum of three sentences about each.

1. A fact that relates to the music artist (about ethnic origin, family history, city in which he/she was born, etc)

Smash Mouth - Steve Harwell: Vocals, Gregory Camp: Guitar & Vocals, Paul Lisle: Bass & Vocals, Kevin Coleman: Drums, Vocals. Steve Harwell says that they aren't any particular Genre, they are a mixture of all kinds of music. The band is from California. Carson Daly (Host of MTV live) helped get their music career started.
Source Internet_____ Page Number_____

2. The subject of the song. For example, "Love Me Tender" by Elvis Presley is about the subject love.

The Sun. The sun is a star. It has 6 areas. The corona, Chromosphere, Convection Zone, Radiation Zone, Core & Photosphere. It would be impossible to walk on the sun, you'd melt before you ever got to the surface. The term "Walkin on the Sun" means that if you break the other or contact, you might a Source New Book of Knowledge Page Number P.441 well be walk on the sun cause they'll kill you.

3. Information relating to a song lyric. For instance, in Elvis' "Jail House Rock", you might research a dance step from the lyric, "Dancing" to the jail house rock.

"Don't delay act now, Supplies are running out"
Usually when supplies run out at a super market, they call & order more. The supplies ship them using those big trailer trailers.

Source_____ Page Number_____

4. Details relating to a musical instrument. ie: guitar, keyboard, piano, etc.

Smash Mouth - Electric Guitar - uses a pick up to amplify sounds. It converts the string sounds to electric impulses. Bass - lowest & largest of the guitar family. Drums - Rock Musicians use different kinds of drums including Bass Drum, Snare Drum, Bongo Drums, & Cymbals
Source New Book of Knowledge_____ Page Number P.411 & 412

5. Discover one fact that all of your group members have in common. To illustrate, all of your group members, that is you and the members in your group, might have blonde hair. Then you might want to research hair.

Me & Andy both wear nikes. Nikes are the most popular shoe in America. They are made in china & cost about $5 to make. They sold here for $70-over $100. They are made by Chinese slaves.

Source_____ Page Number_____

Hannah Walker and Lawrence Baines

Sudden Performance

Type of activity: Group.
Time period: Three 50-minute periods.

Objective

Students learn to do a close reading of a text, discover the nuances of performance and oral delivery, and become acquainted with the format for a script.

Materials

Have four or five copies of several short stories available to the class. Stories from books such as *Sudden Fiction* (Shapard & Thomas, 1986), *Sudden Fiction International* (Shapard & Thomas, 1989), or *Suddenly* (Pelham, 1998) work nicely, though any brief story or scene from a book will work. Make sure that the story you select is appropriate for translation to performance.

Set-Up

Have desks arranged in clusters of three to five. Try to give each group as much space as possible.

Procedure

Place students in groups of three to five.

Explain the project and give each group three short stories from which to choose. The first day, they should read all three stories, then discuss which one they will adapt. They should begin discussing staging, props (if needed), and interpretations of the text. Groups have the freedom to perform extremely faithful or very loose translations. Creative presentations should be encouraged. At the end of the first 50-minute period, ask students to give you the name of the story they will adapt.

In the second 50-minute period, students should begin writing the script and rehearsing. The teacher may want to designate one member of the group as director. Everyone in the group must participate as a writer, actor, or director, or as some combination of the three.

In the third 50-minute period, each group gives a performance. After students present their play, members of the audience write a one- or two-sentence description of the plot and ask questions. The plot summaries should be turned in after everyone has performed.

After the presentations, the teacher may also ask students to write a paragraph or two concerning how performance altered their original conception of the story.

Summary

Sudden Performance may seem straightforward, but it forces students to engage deeply with the text, to consider how the medium affects a message, and to conceptualize and actualize a story through performance.

Enrichment

If a teacher has access to a camcorder, adaptations may be filmed while performed. Videotape seems to work well with students who might otherwise feel hesitant about performing in front of class. To make the activity competitive, have students vote for best adaptation, best actor, and best actress after the performance.

MULTIMEDIA

Lawrence Baines

Online Writing for an E-Zine

Type of activity: Group. Approximate time: Two class periods.

Objective

Students will do much writing in a very short time span. They will learn to write in a variety of styles and be able to identify breaches of tone, plot, and character development.

Materials

This activity works best on a class set of computers that are linked to the Internet, but you can adapt this activity so that it works well with no computers.

Set-Up

Place students in groups of no more than four.

Allow students to read some short, online fiction from each of the online e-zines (online magazines) that you have bookmarked. They should note one e-zine that they find appealing.

Explain to students that they are going to write a collaborative short story that will be submitted to an online publisher the next day.

Procedures

Tell students that they may write in any style they wish, but that every composition should have a unity of theme, style, and tone. Their writing will be timed. When time is called, students should stop writing immediately, get up, and move to the right to sit at the next terminal. Writing will be timed in segments of 3, 4, 5, 6, and 7 minutes. The person who sits down to read the new composition must read what has already been written, do a little thinking, then strive to maintain a consistency of voice, point of view, style, tone, and theme as he or she writes. Everyone in the group writes at least once, so in a group of four there will be four stories at the end of the session.

After the five writing sessions have been completed, students will go through a 10-minute revision process with the composition they worked on last. Revisers should pay special heed to altering aspects of the composition that seem in violation of the style established by the initial writer.

At this point, the groups should have written in six segments—the timed 3-, 4-, 5-, 6-, 7-minute writing episodes, and a 10-minute revision.

Have each student in the group read all the compositions, then vote on the best composition from the group. Next, the most effective oral reader of the group will read the composition aloud to the group, who will listen for consistency of style, tone, theme, and plot and will make revisions to improve the piece. Students often will want to work on editing the best composition out of class.

During the next class period, the students should begin at the computers at the Web site of the publisher of e-zine fiction. They will look at the "calls for manuscripts" or "submission guidelines" sections, then create the necessary documents so that they may submit their stories online. It is best if students make up a name under which they might submit the work. Some groups like to use a conglomeration of parts of everyone's name and identify it as such in their introductory letters.

Summary

Collaborative writing for an online e-zine is an action-packed, fun activity that teaches students about consistency of tone, voice, theme, and point of view without having to complete any worksheets. When I first used this assignment, I had students write and submit their compositions in a single class period just to make writing for publication seem a little less daunting. In order to do this, however, I usually had to interrupt students who were vigorously working on their compositions and tell them to get busy on their letters to editors. Now, I even allow students to take the composition home for revision or to further explore online publication possibilities.

Enrichment

Use computers and online e-zines with this activity to add a sense of urgency and allow closure within the classroom. Of course, a teacher could use this activity without computers by having students sit in a circle and pass their writing, rather than moving to a different computer terminal. Then the submissions might go to publishers who print student work, of which there are a growing number.

Lawrence Baines

Spin Doctors and Truth

**Type of activity: Group.
Approximate time: Works best over
5 to 7 days.**

Objective

Students will learn to discern fact from opinion, will discover ways to manipulate language to achieve specific ends, will become acquainted with some distinguishing features of various media, and will learn to be discriminating media consumers.

Materials

Videotapes, audiotapes, transcripts, pens, and paper.

Set-Up

Take a recent event that has received much media attention. For example, events related to the accusations of U.S. President Bill Clinton's impropriety would have worked well during 1998–1999. Videotape two of the national networks' coverage of the event, as well as the coverage by local television stations. Collect the local newspaper and any other newspaper you can locate, preferably from different geographic regions. Also, record radio news segments from National Public Radio and a commercial radio station, and gather magazines such as *U.S. News and World Report*, *Time*, and *Newsweek* that contain stories on the topic.

Procedure

Day One

Ask students to discuss how they feel about a recent event that received much media coverage. For example, regarding the charges of corruption against a high-profile political figure, some students might remark, "He's immoral," or "The other party is conspiring against him." After these initial responses, attempt to get the class to identify the facts of the case. As students grapple with the difference between fact and speculation, list student suggestions on the overhead projector or the chalkboard. After students have fin-

ished discussing the list, go over their suggestions and place a star next to each suggestion that seems more speculative than factual. Discuss why some suggestions might not necessarily be factual.

The next part takes some preparation on the part of the teacher, who has already collected various audio, video, and print news reports. You can ask students and the librarian to help record these newscasts, so you don't have to do everything yourself. Once you have placed the materials in different areas of the room, place the students into groups for each area. Each group will be responsible for transcribing the reports. Once they transcribe the reports, students should mark them by underlining facts and highlighting opinions or conjecture. Each group should come up with a ratio of the number of factual versus the number of speculative statements.

Station one: Audiotape of the National Public Radio version of the event (these transcripts are also available for a nominal fee)

Station two: A commercial radio newscast

Station three: A national television newscast

Station four: Another national television newscast

Station five: Another coverage by a nonprint medium—news channels such as CNN or another channel

By the end of class, students must transcribe the newscast, mark it accordingly, and come up with the fact to opinion ratio. Other tasks you might want students to do with the newscasts might include a readability/difficulty analysis, a count of polysyllabic words, a listing of unfamiliar terms, average sentence length, or other analyses. Once students finish the transcription, have them turn it in. Make copies of each group's data to distribute at the beginning of class on day two.

DAY TWO

Allow students some time to prepare a presentation of their results. Give them the copies of their research so that they can hand out their data as they present.

After everyone presents, students should have the data from all five news sources. Ask them to rank the newscasts in order from the highest ratio of fact to opinion to the lowest. Discuss commonalities and differences among the newscasts.

Finally, have students select the most important word in their particular newscast. Ask each group to substantiate with evidence why they consider a particular word to be the most important. Allow students to present and defend their responses.

DAY THREE

As in day one, assign students to groups and have students perform analyses as they did previously

for television and radio newscasts. Possible stations might include

Station one: The local newspaper

Station two: *The New York Times* (or *The Wall Street Journal*)

Station three: *Newsweek* (or *Time* or *U.S. News and World Report*)

Station four: *The Weekly Standard* (or *National Review*)

Station five: *National Enquirer* (or any other similar tabloid)

Ask students to complete their transcriptions and analyses by the end of the period so that you can distribute the results to the rest of the class on day four.

DAY FOUR

Follow the same format as in day two, in which you make copies of students results, which each group presents to class.

DAY FIVE

Instruct students to write a paper in class about what they learned about fact, opinion, and media spin. Ask students to attach their transcriptions to their papers.

MULTIMEDIA

Summary

Students seem to enjoy scrutinizing the media and discovering the nuances of words and delivery. Although the set-up may seem overly complex, the rewards of doing this activity are worth the extra set-up time.

Enrichment

The next step in the process is to give students a set of facts and a transcription of an interview, then have them write stories for radio, television, and print based on these inputs. I give each group the same set of information. Each group must produce an actual script and perform the activity accordingly. For example, the group doing the radio spot must record their newscast on audiotape and play it for the rest of class on presentation day.

Group one: 1-minute radio news spot

Group two: 2-minute television news spot

Group three: Front-page newspaper story

Group four: Feature piece in a magazine such as *Time* (or whatever magazine they choose)

Group five: Sensationalistic feature piece in the *National Enquirer* or a similar tabloid.

Lawrence Baines

Performance Art Poetry

Type of activity: Individual poem. Approximate time: 45 minutes (add a few hours if you decide to pursue the enrichment activity).

Objective

Students will use writing prompts to create a dense, eloquent poem about their hometown.

Materials

Pen and paper or computer with word processor.

Set-Up

Begin class by asking students informally about where they grew up. You might want to ask for a show of hands on how many students were born and grew up in the city or town in which they are living now. Allow students to reminisce and tell stories. The idea is to get words flowing.

Procedure

Tell students that they are going to write a poem about their hometowns. Hand out the sheet of instructions and do the first few lines as a class. Emphasize that poetry should be expressive and descriptive.

Hometown:

place where you grew up and a verb (2 words)

the landscape (4 words)

smell or taste of your hometown (6 words)

music, song, or sounds that remind you of your hometown (8 words)

kind of people who live there (10 words)

an important event in your life (12 words)

an important event in your life (12 words—you may repeat the above line or write a new one)

a dream or nightmare (10 words)

an influential person (8 words)

the specific advice or truth someone once gave you (perhaps you heard it from the person mentioned above). Try to write out their advice specifically, then delete the quotations marks. (6 words)

the weather (4 words)

your hometown plus an adjective (2 words)

Summary

Performance Art Poetry provides some structure for students who otherwise might not participate fully in writing poetry or in selecting vibrant, descriptive words.

Enrichment

To do any enrichment activities, a teacher should wait until *after* the writing has been completed. Once the poem has been written, a teacher may want to have students compile photographs, sounds, drawings, words, and images into PowerPoint software presentations. Encourage students to recite their poems to music; either allow them to bring in their own music or allow them to select from music you bring to class. The resulting PowerPoint presentations often result in multimedia performance art.

PERFORMANCE ART POETRY STUDENT SAMPLE

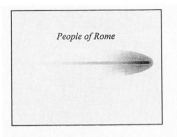
People of Rome

Rome,
Teaches,
stinks and
has three
rivers and
seven hills.

Moving to a new school, older people, new teachers and making new friends...

Starting a new job, co-workers are fun to be around, hospitals are GROSS...

. Nasty school food, funky, and good water

Alarm clock and car horns...

Took a lot of money, hid it in my room, woke up looking for it and felt stupid

• Donna, Scott, my mother who is evil and loves to party...

Mamma's voice and telephone ringing

• Loud, kind, scary and rough, crazy fighting and throwing tvs, clothing...

Nothing in the world is FREE...

• Winter, cold, rainy, ICY old ROME...

What the young writer needs to do, of course, is study sentences, consciously experiment with them, since he can see for himself what the difficulty is, and can see for himself when he has beaten it: Where variety is lacking, sentences all run to the same length, carry over and over the same old rhythms, and have the same boring structure.

Gardner, J. (1985). *The art of fiction* (p. 99). New York: Vintage.

SENTENCE STRUCTURE

MICHAEL, THE 14-YEAR-OLD BOY WHOSE FEET SEEM TO GET IN THE WAY OF HIS EVERY STEP, walks rather hesitantly toward your desk. He's holding his rough draft of the personal essay he is doing for an initial writing sample. As he hands it to you, he lingers a moment, watching you closely, then sort of blurts out that he really doesn't know what to write about. It's obvious to you that he's proud of what he's done, but nervous that you'll point out its flaws. You nod, smile, and begin reading his draft. It doesn't take long to realize that there is no punctuation. Michael is trying not to look nervous as he watches you. You start over, trying to think of something nice to say.

As you read Michael's essay, you wonder where do you begin teaching writing? He's in the ninth grade and should know how to write a sentence. Because this is the first writing sample for the class, you worry about how many more of these kids cannot write a complete sentence. Do you start by explaining the difference between a fragment and a run-on sentence? You hand back the draft to Michael without shattering his feelings and begin to sort through the papers from the class. Over and over you see fragments, run-ons, and a serious weakness in basic sentence structure. The few students who are actually writing complete sentences seem very content writing nothing more daring than a simple subject-verb pattern. You realize that at this level you are going to need to back up quite a bit simply to reach a starting point where you can begin working on some basics.

Activity	Entry point	Students work on	Preparation time needed
Hide the Adjective	Game	Parts of speech	Minimal
Rapid Transitions	Game	Transitions	Minimal
Scrambled Sentences	Story puzzle	Paragraph organization	Substantial
Writing Down the Clincher	Compelling piece of writing	Sentence rhythm	Minimal
Sentence Reversal	A piece of poor writing	Revision	Minimal

You had hoped to try some new ideas with this class, but the things you had in mind require a fundamental understanding of sentences. Now with an increasing sense of dread, you begin to wonder how much time you will need to spend going over what should have been learned in elementary school. What you really need is to engage your students to their maximum potential, to find an unconventional way of creating a basic understanding of sentences. You make a decision: Textbooks will need to stay on the shelf for awhile. It's time to try something new, time to rattle some cages, time to make sentence structure intellectually stimulating, and—dare you think it—fun.

Anthony Kunkel

Hide the Adjective

Type of activity: Cooperative groups of three to four students. Approximate time: One 50-minute class period.

Preamble

    This activity is equally effective using nouns, adverbs, verbs, prepositional phrases, adverbial phrases, and other parts of speech. Hide the Adjective is an activity that can be used to teach not only adjectives, but a variety of skills across the curriculum. For a 50-minute class of 25 students, it is recommended that 20 minutes be left for reading the stories.

Objective

Students will identify adjectives and use them in writing, learn to use descriptive adjectives in sentences, use and increase listening skills through active engagement, and learn creative sentence structure and writing techniques.

Materials

Index cards or small slips of paper big enough to hold a written word (and definition if no dictionaries are available).

Set-Up

One adjective will be needed for each student in the class. It is best to select colorful and interesting adjectives to bring forth some interesting and colorful sentences. For instance, the word *gargantuan* would probably produce a more colorful sentence than the word *big*. On each slip of paper write one adjective (and its definition if no dictionary is available).

Procedure

After a brief discussion of adjectives, give each student one of the slips of paper containing an adjective. It is important to explain to the students ahead of time that if any of their classmates see their adjective, one point could be taken from them. Once students have their adjective in hand, hidden from all eyes, instruct them to write a half-page story using their adjective somewhere in that story. Before the stories are written, inform the students that their stories will be read aloud by the teacher, and the class will be given three attempts to guess the adjective that was assigned for that particular story. Their adjective should be circled or underlined in the story. The object is for writers to be creative as possible and try to hide their adjective within the story, which means they will need to use other adjectives as often as possible. Only one adjective per sentence is allowed, so each student should strive to use as creative an adjective as possible at every opportunity. Once students begin listening to the stories being read, many will immediately wish they had used better adjectives, and this opens the activity to unlimited possibilities for the next time it's used.

Summary

Instantly, students will recognize the need to seek out and use words that they otherwise would not have attempted. It will quickly become evident that not only are students enjoying themselves and beginning to take more pride in their written products, but they are also producing writing that is more sophisticated.

Assessment

Applying a grade to this activity is ultimately up to the teacher. It has been effective to use points as extra credit; this not only gives the students motivation and instant feedback, but also allows the teacher the opportunity to give points or a grade as each story is read aloud. Points are scored two ways. First, when a student raises his hand and correctly guesses his peer's adjective, he receives one point. Second, if no one guesses an adjective within three tries, the writer of that story receives one point. To keep the same students from getting all the points, it is recommended that the teacher call on different students whenever possible, and that each student be allowed a maximum amount of points possible (usually 3 guessing points and 1 point for successfully hiding their adjective).

Enrichment

Block off a week for this activity and begin with something simple like Hide the Noun. After doing this activity once, most students realize that they could have done a better job hiding their word, and they look forward to playing again. The next day follow up with Hide the Adjective, and the results will be pleasantly surprising. Not only will the students do a much better job at hiding their word, but the level of their writing will increase and the stories will become more entertaining. By the end of the week, most students will have become adept at listening and using creative sentences to mask what would otherwise be an obvious word or phrase. The engagement of the students to write creatively while targeting specific skills, and the repetition of listening, identifying, and repeating these target words, has proven in my classes to be more effective for retention than any grammar book on the market.

SENTENCE STRUCTURE

Anthony Kunkel

Rapid Transitions

Type of activity: Cooperative groups of three or four students. Approximate time: One 50-minute class period.

Objective

Students will learn to identify transitions, will demonstrate the use of transitions to connect sentences and ideas, and will realize how to create unity in writing.

Materials

Chalkboard or overhead projector.

Set-Up

Write a large variety of transitional words and phrases on the chalkboard or overhead. The following are some of the transitions I have used in the past:

However	In spite of	Nevertheless
Consequently	Be that as it may	Subsequently
Moreover	In addition to	For example
First off	As a result of	Not only
However	Finally	On the other hand

Procedure

After a brief explanation of transitions and their uses, instruct all groups to get paper ready and listen closely. Each group member should select a number between 1 and 7 and write that number on a piece of paper; no group member should select the same number as anyone else in the group. Once members have selected a number, tell them to listen for their number as you call them so they may write their role assignments next to it. Using the role assignments that follow, call out each number, read the corresponding role assignment, and instruct any student who wrote that number to write their role assignment next to it:

1. Describe the proper way to eat an ice cream cone on a hot day.

2. Give instructions on the best way to ask someone out on a date.

3. Describe what the world will be like in the year 3000.

4. Convince the world that cheerleading should be an Olympic sport.

5. Tell what gift you should get for your graduation and why you should get it.

6. Convince the United States that there would be less violence if everybody carried a gun.

7. Describe a dress that you have just seen in the mall, and tell why you'd look good wearing it.

Once all students have their role assignments written down and understood, they should then designate one person in the group as the beginning writer, who will begin writing an essay on their assigned role topic. Instruct them to treat it as a regular essay, but to write two sentences *only* and then pass the paper to the left within their group. The next student to receive the essay should use one of the transitions from the chalkboard to bring the topic into their assigned role, and then write one more sentence on their assigned role. This same procedure should continue until all the transitions from the board have been used, or you wish to stop the writing.

Summary

Although much of this activity is based on connecting completely unrelated ideas, the students usually will select the best transition available to connect them. I make a point of including oral presentations of the essays immediately after they are completed. Expect laughter, especially when the school's star quarterback describes his dress, but sometimes these unrelated ideas almost seem to fit when connected with a good transition.

Enrichment

After this activity, sometimes I ask students to list several related facts on the chalkboard. Then I ask the students to use the same transitions from the previous activity to put the facts together into one condensed essay of no more than a paragraph or two.

Lawrence Baines

Scrambled Sentences

Type of activity: Individual or groups of two to four students. Approximate time: 15–25 minutes.

Objective

Students will use their knowledge of paragraph organization, sentence structure, logic, and the use of transitions to assemble a group of sentences into a cohesive paragraph.

Materials

Scrambled Sentences handout, pen and paper or computer.

Set-Up

Write the following words on the board:

Ready, fire! Aim.

Ask students what is wrong with this sequence of words. Discuss the importance of ordering information. Ask students for examples of bad organization.

Procedure

Distribute the Scrambled Sentences handout (see facing page), and ask students to rearrange the sentences into a coherent and comprehensible paragraph. Tell students to use as many context clues as possible. Give them a time limit of 10–15 minutes and monitor their progress.

After they have completed the unscrambling, ask students to share their responses. Inevitably, students will differ on their ordering of the sentences. Ask students to defend their ordering with reference to specific context clues and logical flow of content.

Once students have shared and a consensus of opinion is reached, hand out the actual passage. Compare the actual passage to the consensus opinion of sentence sequence and get individual opinions. Discuss the similarities or differences, and try to explain the rationale for the writer's decisions.

Summary

Scrambled Sentences is a short but very useful activity that requires students to consider transitions, context clues, and sentence rhythm.

Enrichment

The next step is to have students use one of their own paragraphs as fodder for scrambling. Once a student scrambles his sentence, he can exchange papers with a peer. As above, the peer attempts to order the sentences into a paragraph. When the student's guess at order is compared against the actual writing, often the writer realizes that his composition lacks a sense of logical progression and internal context clues. As a result, this activity can sometimes substantially enrich the overall quality of student writing.

SCRAMBLED SENTENCES HANDOUT

"MY SON, A GENTLE GIANT, DIES" BY MICHAEL GARTNER

Place the following sentences so that they make the best sense.

1. "If God had come to you 17 years ago and said, 'I'll make you a bargain. I'll give you a beautiful kid for 17 years, and then I'll take him away,'" Tim said, "you would have made that deal in a second."

2. He knew that, he said, and then argued, almost persuasively, how the tree was to blame.

3. He hit a tree the day he got his license.

4. Yet his friend, Tim Russert of NBC, called Friday, devastated as we all are, and said the only thing that has helped.

5. As a parent, you live in fear your child will die in a car wreck, and in his year and a half of driving Christopher did manage to wreck all four of our family cars.

6. We just didn't know the terms.

7. But, it was a sudden, initial attack of juvenile diabetes that killed him, that killed him despite medical heroics and fervid prayers.

8. "It wasn't my fault, Dad." "Well, Christopher," I said, "it was yours or the tree's."

9. And last spring he backed one of my cars into another of my cars, which must be a record of sorts.

10. And that was the deal.

11. It is awful and horrible and sad, and no words can comfort his four grandparents, his brother and sister, his friends or his parents.

12. He announced his other accident to me over the phone by beginning, "Dad, you know those air bags stink when they go off."

(From Farrell, Ed and Jim Miller (Eds.) (1997). *The Perceptive I.* (pp. 173–174). Lincolnwood, IL: National Textbook Company.)

Lawrence Baines

Writing Down the Clincher

Type of activity: Individual or groups of two to four students. Approximate time: 20–30 minutes.

Objective

Students will use their knowledge of sentence rhythm and effective writing to compose a clincher sentence for a piece of writing.

Materials

Write the Clincher handout (see page 50), pen and paper or computer.

Set-Up

Show students an example of some solid writing with an effective clincher sentence.

Here is an excerpt from Scott Russell Sanders' "Under the Influence."

> Work has become an addiction for me, as drink was an addiction for my father. Knowing this, my daughter gave me a placard for the wall: WORKAHOLIC. The labor is endless and futile, for I can no more redeem myself through work than I could redeem my father. I still panic in the face of other people's anger, because his drunken temper was so terrible. I shrink from causing sadness or disappointment even to strangers, as though I were still concealing the family shame. I still notice every twitch of emotion in the faces around me, having learned as a child to read the weather in faces, and I blame myself for their least pang of unhappiness or anger. In certain moods I blame myself for everything. *Guilt burns like acid in my veins.*

(In Farrell, Ed & Jim Miller (Eds.), (1997). *The Perceptive I* (p. 40). Lincolnwood, IL: National Textbook Company.)

Procedure

In this excerpt, the italicized sentence is the clincher. Discuss with students how a clincher is set up. Count the syllables of the sentences leading up to the clincher, then describe how the sentence structure varies. Ask students to list some characteristics about the clincher.

Hand students the Write the Clincher handout, which contains an excerpt from Truman Capote's "A Christmas Memory." Have students write their own clincher for this passage.

Ask students to read some of their clincher sentences aloud. Discuss the qualities of an effective clincher, vote on the two or three best student examples, and analyze the specific traits that make a clincher effective.

Read Truman Capote's clincher sentence:

> As if I expected to see, rather like hearts, a lost pair of kites hurrying toward heaven.

Summary

Sentence rhythm is a delicate skill to learn, though desperately needed among budding writers. Any teacher who has read 15 subject-verb-noun sentences back-to-back realizes the importance of writing effective clincher sentences.

Enrichment

Have students find short stories in contemporary magazines or books and lead a classroom discussion of sentence rhythm. Bring bongo drums or a snare drum and have one student read a passage while another keeps the beat.

WRITE THE CLINCHER HANDOUT

"A Christmas Memory" by Truman Capote

This is our last Christmas together.

Life separates us. Those who Know Best decide that I belong in a military school. And so follows a miserable succession of bugle-blowing prisons, grim, reveille-ridden summer camps. I have a new home, too. But it doesn't count. Home is where my friend is and there I never go.

And there she remains, puttering around the kitchen. Alone with Queenie. Then alone. ("Buddy," she writes in her wild, hard-to-read script, "yesterday Jim Macy's horse kicked Queenie bad. Be thankful she didn't feel much. I wrapped her in a Fine Linen sheet and rode her in the buggy down to Simpson's pasture where she can be with all her Bones....") For a few Novembers she continues to bake her fruitcakes singlehanded; not as many, but some: and, of course, she always sends me "the best of the batch." Also, in every letter she encloses a dime wadded in toilet paper: "See a picture show and write me the story." But gradually in her letters she tends to confuse me with her other friend, the Buddy who died in the 1880s more and more, thirteenths are not the only days she stays in bed: a morning arrives in November, a leafless, birdless coming of winter morning, when she cannot rouse herself to exclaim: "Oh, my, it's fruitcake weather!"

And when that happens, I know it. A message saying so merely confirms a piece of news some secret vein had already received, severing from me an irreplaceable part of myself, letting it loose like a kite on a broken string. That is why, walking across a school campus on this particular December morning, I keep searching the sky.

(From Farrell, E. & Miller, J. (Eds.). (1997). *The perceptive I* (pp. 250–259). Lincolnwood, IL: National Textbook Company.)

Directions

Capote wrote one last sentence. You write one and we'll compare it to the author's.

Lawrence Baines

Sentence Reversal

Type of activity: Individual.
Approximate time: 15 minutes.

Objective

The purpose of this activity is to get students to identify and remedy some of their awkward writing. That is, students identify and rebuild weak sentences.

Materials

Pen and paper or a computer with a word processing program.

Set-Up

Students need to have a draft of a paper that they have written recently in front of them. Have them identify some sentences that just don't seem to work or sentences that they just don't like. Students should highlight or underline no more than two sentences in their papers.

Procedure

Pair students with a reliable partner. Instruct students to read their pieces aloud to their partners, without divulging which sentence they see as weak, and have the partners guess which sentences writers consider weak.

Ask students to reverse their presentations in their sentence. For example, a student may have written the sentence "He no longer cared about the silly details of high school life."

A reversal of this sentence might yield a sentence such as "He pledged to himself to begin caring about his life outside of high school." Another example is "Students at this school are powerless over the decisions that affect their everyday lives."

It can be reversed to read "A student at this school has about as much power as a gnat in the web of a black widow spider."

Summary

Sentence reversals are wonderful ways of overcoming writer's block in relation to sentences that just do not seem to work as they are written originally.

Enrichment

A nice follow-up activity is to get students to reverse sentences from famous quotes. For example, "It was the best of times, it was the worst of times," might turn into "It wasn't a time of celebration or mourning."

Language is the pliable adhesive that helps to form, identify, and bind nations, communities, neighborhoods, groups, societies, and personal relationships. Language is also the means by which those groups give voice to their ideas, dreams, despairs, hopes, fears, memories of yesterday, and visions of tomorrow.

Andrews, L. (1993). *Language exploration and awareness* (p. xv). White Plains, NY: Longman.

ENRICHING VOCABULARY

You cringe as the supervising teacher points to the 20 vocabulary words on the chalkboard. You saw them when you came in and remembered what it was like being in high school and experiencing those endless lists of vocabulary words. You are not surprised when the students are given the assignment. After all, it's a Monday. "Write them down, take them home, look them up, write a definition, use them in a sentence, and bring them back tomorrow," says the teacher. You wonder who invented this technique as the standard for learning vocabulary.

As the students turn in their vocabulary assignments the next day, they are handed a test asking them to match definitions to words and words to definitions. You notice that most of them did the homework and acknowledge that most will pass the test, yet you feel relatively certain that few students will remember any of these words beyond next week.

This is the class that you are taking over in a few days—the first time in your student-teaching experience that you'll be teaching alone. Vocabulary to these students is simply one throw-away day per week, part of the gauntlet they must run if they want to pass. The vocabulary words have little meaning to them. They are simply linguistic placebos to be carried for a limited time within their short-term memories.

Activity	Entry point	Students work on	Preparation time needed
Vocab War	Game	Increasing vocabulary	Substantial
Thinking Sentences	Game	Using vocabulary words in context	Minimal
Word Bingo	Game	Vocabulary	Substantial
Living the Word	Skit	Pronunciation and retention of meaning	Minimal
Synonym Scuffle	Game	Synonyms	Minimal

The dreariness of vocabulary study is unnerving—words are the soul of the English language arts. You know the students desperately need to learn words, to learn the value of words, and you also know that most of them don't realize it. Somehow, you need to revitalize the study of language so that students will look forward to learning vocabulary, not dread it.

Anthony Kunkel

Vocab War

Type of activity: Cooperative groups of three or four students. Approximate time: One 50-minute class period.

Preamble

When first developed, Vocab War was intended to be used primarily as an occasional break from the traditional vocabulary approach of having students look up a list of words, write definitions, and then use the words in a context sentence. What quickly became apparent after playing this game weekly for several weeks was that not only were students remembering the key vocabulary words and using them in class, but students looked forward to playing and were becoming experts at using dictionaries. With each week the game became more successful, as did the need to establish some clearly defined rules of play. Listed with this activity are the rules and rewards I have developed during the 4 years I have been using it. These rules are only suggested, but have proven to be successful in maximizing the learning potential for this game.

Objective

Students will increase vocabulary, learn cognitive reasoning skills, uncover analogous relationships, become proficient in all uses of the dictionary, learn to use synonyms and antonyms, and increase spelling and pronunciation skills.

Materials

A dictionary of synonyms and antonyms (found in any bookstore), a chalkboard (the larger the better), and a set of dictionaries.

Set-Up

Use the dictionary of synonyms and antonyms to select five words that are appropriate for the level of class. Select three synonyms and three antonyms to go with each of these five words. For example, in the game that follows, the word *zeal* was selected. With this word are the synonyms *fervor*, *haste*, and *spirit*,

and antonyms *lethargy*, *apathy*, and *torpor*. The original five words selected will become the key words to the game (these are usually the words I hold the students responsible to learn), and the synonyms and antonyms will be the words the students must match to these key words. On one side of the chalkboard, write the five key words across the top and create a chart similar to the one listed below (listed are five of the key words I have used with my regular ninth-grade English class):

ZEAL		VOLATILE		UNION		TERSE		SINISTER	
S	A	S	A	S	A	S	A	S	A

On the other side of the chalkboard list the synonyms and antonyms that match the five key words in a random order similar to the columns listed below:

pithy	fervor	soluble
inauspicious	junction	buoyant
lethargy	tedious	dispersion
concise	lucky	vapid
division	noxious	apathy
serious	vapory	sublimated
spirit	haste	alliance
laconic	redundant	cumbrous
discord	malign	gracious
coalition	roseate	torpor

Procedure

Part One

Instruct students to use their dictionaries to look up the definitions for the five key words. Once a student has successfully looked up a key word, he or she should write the definition in words they will understand; this first part is essential to the success of each group and the game. Having done this, each group should divide the columns of synonyms and antonyms, and each group member is responsible for looking up the words in his or her designated column.

At this point explain to the groups the process of matching the synonyms and antonyms to the key words. (It is normal for there to be some confusion with the introduction of this activity, but most students will catch on quickly, especially once the game gets going.) As simply as possible, explain that each group member should begin looking up his or her column one word at a time. Once they find the first word of their column, students should consult their written definition of the first key word. It is not necessary for the group member to write any definitions to her column word, but instead, she should compare the dictionary definition against her written definition of the key word. The idea is to look at the two words and reason whether or not they have similar meanings. If the two words clearly have similar meanings, the student should list the column word as a synonym for the key word it matches. But if it does not, she should then consider if the meaning is the opposite of their key word. Once again, if it is clear that the column word belongs under the key word, only as an antonym, it gets listed in the antonym column. If the first word of their column does not fit as a synonym *or* antonym of the first key word, the student should move on to the second key word and repeat the process. Instruct students to repeat these steps until all words in their column have been identified and matched to their proper key words.

Part Two

After all groups have been given half the class period to look up and match synonyms and antonyms, it is time to begin the game. Tell students to continue looking up words when the game begins, but at this point, they also should begin to focus as a group on what words they have matched, what words are being put on the chalkboard by other groups, and what words they still need to match. The game then proceeds as follows:

Select a group to begin. One member of the selected group will then have 60 seconds to go to the chalkboard and write a synonym or antonym in its appropriate column. The groups are not informed if they are correct or not; they simply put a word on the board then take their seats. If the word placed on the board is correct, the group will receive one point, and if it is incorrect, the group will receive no points. Once the first group is finished, it is the second group's turn.

The second group, like the first group, also will have 60 seconds to place a synonym or antonym in its appropriate column, only they first have the option of erasing the first word from the board if they feel it is in the wrong column. In order to do this, they must first pronounce the word correctly and ask permission to erase it. If the word is pronounced incorrectly, whether it is in the right column or not, inform the group member that she has pronounced it wrong and ask her to take her seat; the group's turn is forfeited. If the word is pronounced correctly but is in the right column, inform the group member that the word is correct where it is, but she must take her seat; the group's turn is forfeited. If the word is pronounced correctly and is in the wrong column, the group member may erase it and then place any word she wishes under the column she wishes. She does not have to re-place or place the word she has erased. If a group is not certain and does not wish to risk it, the students are not required to identify a misplaced word, but instead may simply use their turn to place a synonym or antonym in the column they feel it belongs.

If a group does correctly identify a misplaced word and then correctly places a word under its correct key word, the group receives 2 points instead of 1. If a group correctly identifies a misplaced word but misplaces the synonym or antonym it chooses to write on the board, the group receives 0 points.

Once the second group has finished its turn at the board, the third group has 1 minute to take its turn. The game proceeds until all the synonyms and antonyms have been correctly placed under their key words, or until time runs out. A competitive class will occasionally finish the game with about 5 minutes to spare during a 50-minute period, which is the same amount of time you should leave for scoring and summary.

To help the game, inform a group to circle a column once it contains the three proper synonyms or antonyms. No points are given for circling a column; it is merely a courtesy to the players to help them identify and concentrate on the remaining words. This will also allow the more competitive groups to focus on identifying a misplaced word under a column that has three words in it and is not circled.

Rules of the Game

- Each group has 60 seconds to take their turn.
- Any word placed on the board that is already in a circled column will result in the loss of 1 point.
- Misspelled words are considered wrong.
- Anyone wishing to erase a word from the board must first ask permission and pronounce the word correctly (including misspelled words).

- No group member may talk to anyone outside of his or her group during the entire course of the game; to do so results in loss of 1 point.

- Group members may correct and talk to their representative member while he or she is at the chalkboard.

- Only one member from each group may go the chalkboard during the group's turn, and each group must rotate who goes with each turn.

- If a group does not have a word to place on the board when it is their turn, they may attempt to erase an incorrect word without having to place a word on the board. No points may be scored for doing this, and the chance for a perfect game is forfeit, but no points are lost for passing.

POINTS AND SCORING

- Students earn 1 point for a word identified and placed under the correct key word.

- Students earn 2 points for correctly identifying, pronouncing, and erasing a word, then placing a word correctly on the board. If a group successfully erases a word but misses the word they place on the board, no points are given.

- If a group plays a perfect game, makes no mistakes and loses no points, its score is doubled.

- A group will lose 1 point if any member talks to anyone outside of the group during the game.

- A group will lose 1 point if it places a word on the board that has already been placed in a column that is circled.

- A group will lose 1 point if it passes when it is its turn.

Summary

Although this game may have started out as a means of broadening my approach to teaching vocabulary, it has evolved into a weekly event that many of my students look forward to. I now keep a scoreboard in my classroom and have my classes battle one another for high score of the week. For added incentive, on the Monday after a game, I test my students on the five key words using a multiple-choice combination of definitions and synonyms from the game, and I exempt my winning class from that test. This has been so successful as a motivator that I now exempt from the test the group with the high score in each of my classes.

Fridays have become Vocab War Day in my classes, and it is completely normal for students to stop in throughout the day to get a jump on the key words so they may come to class ready to begin matching the synonyms and antonyms. In some cases students have even been known to leave a false list of the matched words in their dictionaries, hoping to fool a student coming into the next class period. As a result of this game, many of my students have begun using many of the vocabulary words from the game in their daily conversations. Students also quickly begin showing a willingness and comfort toward using a dictionary for the simplest of assignments—without being told or asked to use one.

Anthony Kunkel

Thinking Sentences

Type of activity: Cooperative groups of three or four students. Approximate time: One 50-minute class period.

Objective

Students will increase vocabulary, use difficult words in context, develop reasoning skills, and demonstrate how to write and use complex sentences.

Materials

Chalkboard and set of dictionaries.

Set-Up

Write a creative prompt on the chalkboard that will help stimulate the writing of a short story. For example

Everything was perfect until the first one fell from the sky.

Next, list several nouns and adjectives on the chalkboard. It is up to you to select words that are suitably challenging for your students. It is also helpful to include the part of speech for each word. The following list is a sample of words I have used with my average ninth graders:

esoteric—*adj*	existential—*adj*	substratum—*n*
phylum—*n*	ironic—*adj*	obstinate—*adj*
placebo—*n*	illusion—*n*	subtle—*adj*
eloquent—*adj*	luminary—*n*	atrocity—*n*

Procedure

Students select a member from their group to begin their short stories. This student is to copy the story prompt from the board, and then follow that prompt with the next two sentences of the story, which come from the student's own imagination. The student must use one of the words from the chalkboard in one of his two sentences, and he must use it correctly in context.

Once the student has written two sentences using one of the vocabulary words in one of them, he should pass the story to the left within the group, and the student receiving the story must add two sentences of his own to the story. He, too, must use one of the vocabulary words within one of his sentences. Students should not select a word that has already been used, and advise students not to add suffixes or prefixes to any of the words, as that may change the part of speech, and the focus of this lesson's objectives would then begin to blur.

Continue the activity until either time runs out or all words from the chalkboard have been used. Inform students that when the story comes around to them, it is their job to check their peers' grammar. If a mistake is found, the reader should return the paper to the person who made the mistake and politely point it out so that it may be fixed.

Summary

This activity has produced some remarkable short stories. Most students enjoy Thinking Sentences, and there is usually a high level of collaboration within each group. It is not uncommon for the students to ask if they can read their stories aloud, and I usually have a person from each group read the stories aloud after everyone has finished. Having the students read their stories aloud is also a clever means to sneak in a lesson on pronunciation and how to use the dictionary.

Enrichment

An idea that has worked well in conjunction with Thinking Sentences is to require students to begin one of their sentences with a subordinating conjunction, which forces them to write a complex sentence, and to use one of the vocabulary words in a second sentence. For example, I might write this on the board:

> As I made my way through the airport crowd to gate 32, I bumped into a wild-eyed, old woman wearing a bright purple sweater.

Next, I might solicit another example from students and write that on the board as well.

Anthony Kunkel

Word Bingo

Type of activity: Individual. Approximate time: One 50-minute class period.

Objective

Students will increase vocabulary skills, learn and demonstrate dictionary skills, organize and write sentences under time constraints, and use difficult words in context.

Materials

Chalkboard or overhead and set of dictionaries.

Set-Up

Select 25 level-appropriate vocabulary words, and write them in random order on a chalkboard or overhead. Listed below is a sample list of words that I have used with an average ninth-grade class:

timid	antipathy	genial	vain	ardent
foray	reverence	modest	ravage	enmity
boastful	pompous	bleak	repair	honor
stoical	plunder	pacifier	shrew	apathetic
esteem	toady	atonement	coy	zealous

Procedure

Instruct all students to draw a bingo sheet of 25 squares or rectangles (5 columns with 5 rows). It is not necessary for students to put numbers or letters on the bingo sheet. Once all students have their bingo sheets ready, instruct them to fill each square on their sheets with one of the words from the chalkboard, in a random order. Students may put words in any square they like as long as they do not use any word twice; recommend to students that they do not copy the words in the order they are written on the board, which will ensure that none of their classmates have the same bingo sheet as them.

After all students have completed their bingo squares, select the first word and call it out; to make the game more ceremonious I usually write the words on little squares of paper and pull them from a box. Students mark the word that was called on their bingo sheets. They then must look up that word, list its part of speech, and use that word properly in a sentence. Inform students that they will have 2 minutes to complete this before the next word is called out. This will continue until a student completes a column of five words and proclaims "Bingo!" When the student calls "Bingo," he or she must read each word from the bingo column, along with the part of speech and the sentence containing that word. If the word is read correctly, the part of speech is right, and the sentence demonstrates the appropriate context for the word, that student has won. If the student incorrectly identifies the part of speech or misuses the word in a sentence, tell her how it was misused as well as the proper use, and explain that the column on her sheet becomes forfeit. Students can fix their error, though, in case that word becomes part of a different column in progress. Then, the game resumes until the next student calls "Bingo!"

Summary

One thing I have found with this game is that students will quickly pick up the proper usage of descriptive words, and their sentences will become colorful and effective—even without a complete understanding of a particular word. Most students are intimidated at first by the restricted time limits, but they quickly become motivated once they have two or three words in a particular column. A small candy bar treat works to motivate those students who need a reason to play. I also give the winner of the game an automatic "A" on the written work if I plan on grading it, which is always an effective motivator for grade-conscious students. If the game ends too quickly, most students will wish to continue for a second- or third-place finish.

Although this is a game I've had a great deal of success with in all my English classes, I cannot take full credit for this idea. It actually began with three boys in one of my ninth-grade skills classes who wanted to invent a game that would make looking up definitions more fun. I've developed the idea into more work than they originally had intended, but every time we played they would remind me that the game was their idea. I thank them for the idea—and for the enthusiasm.

Enrichment

What has also worked well with Word Bingo is teaching terms and vocabulary that are being taught across the curriculum. For instance, a middle school social studies teacher I know uses this game to teach geographic terms. Students are armed with their textbooks and are given words such as *strait*, *fjord*, and *escarpment*, and to the teacher's delight, the students not only began using the words correctly, but also began to understand the geographic concepts that belonged with them.

Lawrence Baines

Living the Word

Type of activity: Individual. Approximate time: Works best over 2 days.

Objective

Students will learn the meanings, spellings, and pronunciations of new words, to retain them, and to integrate them in their daily speech.

Materials

Lists of vocabulary words.

Set-Up

On the first day, give the class a set of vocabulary words. Slowly pronounce the words, then have students say them back to you. Next, assign each student one vocabulary word; you may also wish to pair up students to do a vocabulary word. Say the entire list again, one at a time, with students repeating the words back to you.

Tell students that the next day they will have to *perform* the word in class. Students have to write out the word in letters at least 24 inches high. Then they also should act out a skit to demonstrate the meaning of their word, and draw a large visual that helps illustrate the meaning or pronunciation of the word. Students should try to limit their presentations to 2 minutes.

Procedure

On the second day, students show their word, present the visual associated with their word, and act out a short skit. Of course, students can enlist other classmates as part of a supporting cast.

LIVING THE WORD STUDENT SAMPLE

PAEAN —tribute
—a hymn of thanksgiving

PAEAN

I. VISUAL

OH GREAT APOLLO WE THANK YOU!

OR SHOW A CLIP FROM AN OSCAR PRESENTA-TION OF A LIFE-TIME ACHEIVEMENT AWARD

II. Act Out:
I WOULD PRESENT MY OWN TRIBUTE TO Apollo or Athena to the class. I WOULD WRITE/Sing to a God or Goddess in an effort to have the idea of a PAEAN stick in their minds.

After students perform the skit, they must place their word (remember it is at least 24 inches high) and the associated visual clue somewhere in the room.

Summary

One of the problems with teaching vocabulary is that many students fail to integrate new words into their everyday vocabularies. To overcome this, assign Living the Word on Monday, then students can give their word presentations on Tuesday. By Friday, most students have seen the large words with their respective visual cues on the walls for at least 3 days and usually will do well on a weekly vocabulary exam.

Enrichment

I suggest giving any student who can find the word printed in newspapers, magazines, or books an extra five points on the weekly vocabulary quiz. Sometimes I give students extra points for purposefully interjecting the vocabulary words in the course of the regular school day.

Wendy Vascik

Synonym Scuffle

Type of activity: Cooperative. Approximate time: One 50-minute class period.

Objective

Students will interpret vocabulary for correct usage in writing, translate meanings of challenging vocabulary words, differentiate parts of speech, and vary word choices for specific meanings within writing.

Materials

Chalkboard; previous vocabulary assignments may be helpful.

Set-Up

Divide students into four even groups. Prepare a list of four new vocabulary words.

Procedure

Instruct students to sit in a close circle within their groups. Explain that in Synonym Scuffle all groups will have 90 seconds to make a list of synonyms for each of four words that are called out to them. After the first word has been called out (and 90 seconds have passed), immediately call out the second word. Continue this until all four words have been called out and 6 minutes have passed.

Now each group should arrange themselves so that all members are facing the chalkboard. One representative from each group will then go to the chalkboard and write all of his or her group's synonyms for the first word. Give one point for each correct synonym, and discuss which words are correct and which are not, as well as which words vary in parts of speech. Continue the activity until all words have been mentioned, synonyms have been written and discussed, all points have been tallied, and the winners are announced. Although you may wish to offer baubles as rewards, often the competition proceeds smoothly without any extrinsic motivation.

Note: It may be helpful for scoring if students are reminded that when a synonym replaces a word in a sentence, it must be able to work within that same sentence, and therefore, it must be the same part of speech.

Summary

After the first 90-second competition, the students catch on and momentum picks up. Knowing that they are competing against other groups, the students huddle closely so as not to leak their "more mature" vocabulary. I allow the students to use their previous vocabulary assignments as guides, which encourages them to use these assignments in future writing. Negotiation over words becomes more intense, and the entire class participates. Students leave class with working vocabularies, confidence in using them, and another reference for their notebooks. Aside from using new words in their writing, students often approach me during reading assignments to point out new words they recognize and understand in context.

Enrichment

To emphasize the importance of using varied word choice, the students are assigned creative writings that include several (usually 10) vocabulary words. They are applying the new vocabulary in context and learning to use new words correctly instead of simply memorizing vocabulary words and then forgetting them after the test.

Regular opportunities to engage in activities that use different modes of discourse are...important to student growth. For example, the processes involved in responding to literature differ from those used in seeking information from texts and then presenting it to others. These modes must be taught, modeled, and practiced.

Squire, J. (1995). The language arts. In G. Cawelti (Ed.), *Handbook of research on improving student achievement* (p. 80). Arlington, VA: Educational Research Service.

NONFICTION

DARRELL, A STUDENT OF YOURS WHO BECAME A NATIONAL MERIT SCHOLAR, had never been an eager fiction reader. "Why read stories that are made up?" he'd ask. "There's so much that I don't know about the *real* world." Although he was extremely bright, he preferred math, social studies, and science to English. To Darrell, fiction was not so much boring as irrelevant.

As an English teacher, you know that you are biased in favor of poetry and prose, and you confess that most of your students will not wind up as college English professors. But because scientists, journalists, and historians still communicate mostly with words, you attempt to work with your colleagues in other fields to bring an interdisciplinary approach to your classroom. Indeed many of the best-known authors from the United States—John Steinbeck, Ernest Hemingway, Jack London, William Faulkner, Dorothy Parker, Flannery O'Connor, Toni Morrison, Joan Didion, Jack Kerouac—have written nonfiction at one time or another. You like to give the future scientists in your classes an opportunity to create an elegant scientific report, the historians a chance to write pellucidly about significant historical figures, and the journalists an occasion to research and report with panache.

So you mix it up. You illuminate the diverse cultures in the United States, dig up startling statistics about American life, and provide abundant resources on the environment, sociological trends, and health. Then you turn over the conversation to students by asking, "What does it all mean?" Their conclusions are not as important to you as the logic and eloquence of their arguments.

Activity	Entry point	Students work on	Preparation time needed
Wanted Posters	Photos of prominent African Americans	Research	Substantial (considerable resource gathering)
Same Facts, Different Audiences	Fact sheet of current dilemma	Writing for a specific audience and purpose	Substantial (need to create fact sheet)
Contracting a Disease	Description of disease	Research, understanding of scientific phenomena	Substantial
Teacher spy	Espionage	Adding details	Minimal
History of My Writing	A piece of student writing	Reflection, analysis of how they write	Minimal

Tracie Pullum

Wanted Posters

Type of activity: Group research. Approximate time: 5–7 days.

Objective

Students will recognize influential Americans and their accomplishments in U.S. history, pull information from various resources, organize information using appropriate research skills, write a character sketch of a prominent American, and work cooperatively with another student to create a finished product.

Materials

List of influential Americans from which students may choose
Folders with information about each person on the list

Guided note-taking sheet and model paragraph (I make these up)

Pictures of each person on the list (you may want to have students download photos from the Internet)

Large white construction paper

White paper ($7^1/_2 \times 5^1/_2$)

Colored construction paper

Markers, colored pencils, scissors, glue

Index cards

Two-column note sheet

Procedure

Day One

Pair students and have them choose an influential American from the list, then give each pair a folder with information about their person. Students read the information to each other.

Days Two and Three

Students reread the material in order to take notes with the guided note-taking sheet.

Students work together to produce a character sketch of their subject. They can use the provided model as a guide. Students then create a nickname for their person.

Circulate around the room, read, and give advice to pairs while they are working.

Once you have seen the finished draft, students may write or type their draft neatly on the white paper.

Days Four and Five

Students will finish final drafts, then using the art materials and colored paper, they will create their wanted posters using the instructed layout. (See student sample on page 77.)

Days Six and Seven

Students prepare an oral presentation on index cards from their notes and character sketch, which will include the person's name, nickname, birth date and place, accomplishments, death date and place, and other meaningful information.

Pairs then present their person to the class. Assess students on their ability to speak clearly and to present meaningful information to the class. Students should take notes on their classmates' presentations.

Summary

The Wanted Posters activity brings out creativity in my students that I do not usually see. When paired with the right person, many of those who do not usually focus well work diligently. I believe having the students "buddy read" and take notes together before starting their character sketches results in better final drafts. With a model to refer to, students who get stuck when writing have something to get them started. Having the students present gives them the opportunity to draw information from what they read as well as from what they write because they know they have to take their time and choose the correct things to say in their presentations about their African Americans. Students also take more time and put more effort into their posters because they know that others will see them in the classroom and during their presentation.

Enrichment

Wanted Posters would be an appropriate activity for highlighting specific individuals during Black History Month, Cinco de Mayo, or Women's History Month.

WANTED POSTERS STUDENT SAMPLE

Lawrence Baines

Same Facts, Different Audience

Type of activity: Groups of three or four students, although the activity could be adapted easily for individual work.

Approximate time: 3 days.

Objective

Students will consider how presentation of content, style, voice, and tone affect audience, medium, and purpose.

Materials

Fact sheet concerning a topic of your choice, pen and paper, or a computer with word processor.

Set-Up

Discuss a recent issue of importance, either on your campus or at a school nearby.

Have students make some educated guesses regarding the issue, and write down these guesses.

Procedure

On day one, hand out the Fact Sheet. (You may create your own fact sheet on any topic you wish—school policy, international affairs, environmental issues, or any current "hot topic.") Discuss the Fact Sheet as a class. Explain why the trends and issues represented by the data are important.

Divide students into five or six different groups and distribute the Same Facts, Different Audience sheet. (See page 80 for a sample that could accompany a Fact Sheet about school or societal violence.)

By the end of the day, each group should write down and hand in to you the three projects on which they would like to work. Make sure that the work load is evenly distributed within the group by asking students to designate one individual as the person responsible for completion of each task. Thus, although students work together, within each group one student coordinates the completion of one of the three projects.

Once students finish their projects (usually by the third day), they should present their results to the rest of class. As each group makes its presentation, the rest of the class should assess the degree to which each project achieved its desired goal.

After all groups have presented, have students analyze the different kinds of appeals that were used within categories. For example, what kinds of techniques were used in attempting to persuade a resistant audience?

Summary

Not only do students gain knowledge about current issues of the world, they learn how audience, purpose, and medium help determine content, tone, style, and voice.

Enrichment

You may request that students do projects individually. You also might have a variety of fact sheets available so that students may choose among a variety of topics.

SAME FACTS, DIFFERENT AUDIENCE

Please select one from each of the three groups:

1. Writing for an adolescent and adult audience:
   a. Create a survey concerning student fears and perceptions of violence at your school. Contrast the results with national data.
   b. Write a letter to the editor of a local newspaper, a news feature story, or a column for the student newspaper commenting on the role of violence in contemporary life.
   c. Write a fictional short story that should persuade someone to take action to halt the proliferation of violence in schools.

2. Writing for a young audience in a predominantly visual medium:
   a. Create a television commercial suitable for airing on Saturday morning that alerts young children to the danger of guns.
   b. Create a poster alerting young children to the danger of guns suitable for hanging in the hallways of an elementary school.
   c. Design a Web page that would alert elementary-age children to some of the dangers of guns, as well as inform them about some relevant statistics.

3. Writing for a resistant audience:
   a. Write a letter to the National Rifle Association asking it to endorse a statewide ban on automatic weapons and handguns.
   b. Find fault with several of the statistics. Write a response to the National Center for Education Statistics identifying aspects of the data that you consider tainted, sensationalistic, or inaccurate. Support why you think that the data are negative and give some idea as to the legitimate figures.
   c. You are representing the United States in a junior United Nations. Several countries, most notably representatives from France, Japan, Iraq, and Sudan, cite the prevalence of violence in schools as evidence that Americans are genetically more violent than citizens from other countries. You want to combat their views by presenting data in such a way that these individuals will no longer perceive of violence in schools as evidence of an American predisposition for violence.

Jan Miller

Diagnosing Symptoms: An Exercise in Critical Thinking

**Type of activity: Individual.
Approximate time: A minimum of
two 50-minute classes in the media
center.**

Objective

   Students will assimilate facts into a cohesive essay, write from specific
perspectives, and assume identities of people with actual genetic or hereditary
disorders. They will write for the purpose of giving information.

Materials

List of health conditions, fact sheet, media center (Internet access would be helpful), and access by phone or letter to support groups for specified disorders.

Set-Up

None needed.

Procedure

Give students a list of suitable disorders on which the school media center has sufficient information to conduct research. Conduct a short summary discussion of each disorder, eliciting and answering questions. After each student has selected one specific disorder to research, hand out a fact sheet on which they can fill in facts on each specific disorder. (See facing page for a sample fact sheet.) Students are then to gather as much information about their selected disorder as possible, and will proceed to write an informative essay about the disorder from the first-person point of view. Instruct students to assume the role of either a person with the disorder or a parent of a child with the disorder, and write their essay from this perspective, telling all they can about the disorder.

Summary

The majority of the students doing this activity become extremely involved with the research, so much so that much of their information comes from searching the Internet and other sources outside of the classroom. Many of the students are extremely creative in their approach to the assignment, and essays usually indicate empathy for the victims of such inescapable conditions.

Enrichment

Given more time, this would be an excellent assignment on which to conduct oral presentations. Also, this activity originated as an extension of a study of Mendelian and chromosomal inheritance in a tenth-grade biology class, and it would be a good opportunity for an interdisciplinary unit.

FACT SHEET

1. Name of disorder _____

2. Cause of disorder _____

3. Symptoms _____
_____
_____

4. In what group of people does this disorder most often occur? _____
_____

5. Prognosis for the disorder _____
_____

6. Treatment _____
_____
_____

7. Recent developments or research _____
_____
_____
_____

8. Can the disorder be detected before birth? How? _____
_____

9. How often does the disorder occur in a population? _____
_____

10. Other facts (What famous person might have had it? How did it get its name? etc.)
_____
_____
_____

Lawrence Baines

Teacher Spy

Type of activity: Individual. Approximate time: 2-week set-up, and two 50-minute writing periods.

Objective

Students will use skills of observation, a variety of descriptive writing techniques, and explicit detail to characterize a teacher at the school.

Materials

Pen and paper.

Set-Up

Two weeks before the class is to begin writing, ask students to begin tracking the habits of one particular teacher at school in a journal. In general, students seem to enjoy the "detective" aspect of this assignment. Students should attempt to include observations of at least the following aspects of the teacher, though they may record their observations in any format they wish.

teacher's choice of clothing

facial features, including hair styles and colors

favorite expressions or words, including a description of the teacher's voice

typical interactions with students

some likely aspirations or dreams of the teacher

where the teacher might be or what he or she might be doing in 10 years

any other unique features or distinguishing characteristics of the teacher

Students should write out responses to these observations at the conclusion of their 2-week journal assignment and before beginning the character sketch. Your initial check of these responses should focus on the explicitness of their recorded observations. For example, "He was a big guy" should not be allowed. Rather, "He was so tall that he had to duck his head as he stepped into the room after the tardy bell rang."

Procedure

Students then write a character sketch from the details that they recorded about a teacher, using their individual journals and their responses to the seven points mentioned earlier. Students should change the name of the teacher they describe. Most papers should have at least five paragraphs.

Once students think that they have a finished draft, they should get at least three of their peers to critique it. The peers should

guess the identity of the teacher,

give at least one additional detail about the teacher that the author did not note,

give their impression of the teacher, especially if it differs radically from the description they are reading, and

assess the degree of detail in the description and offer suggestions for improvement.

After the peer edit, instruct authors to revise at their discretion. In addition to the changes suggested by their peers, which may or may not be heeded, special attention should be given to the final paragraph. A final paragraph should draw from new data offered by peers or should wrap-up or give a new twist to the description.

Summary

In many ways, having students write about teachers at their school is easier than asking students to write fictional stories out of the blue. First, the blank page does not impede students. Instead, they have pages of journal notes and a response sheet from which to draw. Second, writing about a real teacher has the added advantage of being relevant in a visceral way to the students' lives. Not surprisingly, sometimes students use the character sketch to vent their negative feelings about a particular teacher or to glorify a teacher they admire. Either way, it makes for lively writing.

Enrichment

An enlightening follow-up assignment is to have students write a character sketch about themselves from the teacher's perspective, using the same guidelines as they used for the character sketch of the teacher.

TEACHER SPY STUDENT SAMPLE

She was a permanent feature of the school; she had been there for as long as anyone could remember. Every student knew, deep in his heart, that she would never retire; when she was 105 she would still croak from her hospital bed, "If you have permission to talk, stand up beside your seat."

She was a short, dumpling-like thing and looked perfectly harmless to the casual observer. But to those who appeared in class every morning, she was a holy terror.

She had greyish-white hair, short and permed. Her gold-rimmed glasses sat forever atop her head. Her large nose sat squarely amid fleshy, flabby jowls and a small pursed mouth that resembled a child's after tasting a lemon. She was always in style—last year's.

She invariably asked impossible questions that demanded impossible answers, while her steely brown eyes just dared the person asked to attempt a response.

Her voice was high, piercing, and nasal and caused the bursting of more than a few eardrums. Nevertheless everyone slept. Eyelids began to droop until the Texan accent rose a pitch higher and brought sleepy heads wide awake.

Still, for all her faults, she is probably the one teacher I had who actually taught me about the beauty of mathematics, the joy of knowing that one correct answer exists somewhere out there in the universe. She taught me that the amount of suffering one goes through in solving a problem is usually proportional to the value of what has been learned. Kind of like life. It seemed such an ugly lesson at the time, but now I think I understand.

Cara Livingstone Turner and Irving Seidman

The History of My Writing

NONFICTION

Type of activity: Individual with an audience of peers.
Approximate time: 2–3 days.

Preamble

Writing is a developmental activity. It has a history that either has been nourished, ignored, or inhibited. When English and language arts teachers are aware of their own history of writing, they may become more thoughtful about the stories that their students bring to their classrooms.

The idea of reconstructing one's historical experiences with writing is grounded in a combination of two methods of qualitative research. The first is in-depth interviewing from a phenomenological perspective (Seidman, 1998). The goal of this type of research is to help a person reconstruct his or her experience about the topic of desired study, in this case writing. In order for a researcher to understand a person's experience, he or she must place that experience in context, which the researcher attains by conducting a series of three in-depth interviews, respectively centering on one's life history, current experiences, and the meaning of the experiences. Part of this assignment requires each student to research (interview) himself or herself by writing about his or her history of writing and learning to write.

The second research method that forms this writing assignment is ethnography. Ethnography involves the portrayal of everyday experiences through narrative and descriptive observation. For example, a researcher investigating the behavior of air traffic controllers would hang out in the control tower of an airport for a length of time, all the while recording the interactions among the workers and describing their work environment. Recently, composition theorists such as Linda Brodkey (1996) have written about ethnographic research they have conducted on their own lives. These writers immerse themselves in researching their own lives to gain a better understanding of their writer identity, and the final products are called *autoethnographies*. Brodkey and others who write autoethnographies use ethnographic research methods to trace their histories and document their experiences. Once students have "interviewed" themselves about their past histories with writing, we ask them to interview others, collect historical artifacts that represent them as writers, and "observe" their experiences with writing.

Objective

Students will learn that writing has a social and political history, and they will generate principles for teaching writing based on their own social and political histories of writing and learning to write.

Materials

A written explanation of the assignment.

"Writing relics" that students will bring and share with the class. (Writing relics are pieces of writing from the students' past. For example, some students may want to bring in their favorite essay from third grade.)

Set-Up

Go over the explanation of the assignment. Spend some time talking about phenomenology and autoethnography.

Procedure

Explain the Assignment

Students will write a paper that recreates the history of their experiences with writing. Their assignment is to answer the question, "What has writing been like for you up until this point in your life?"

Encourage students to become ethnographic researchers by talking with parents, siblings, former teachers, and friends about their early writing practices and also by searching for and revisiting samples of their former writing and other writing relics. They may gain a richer picture of their own writing history by exploring the writing histories of their parents, guardians, or grandparents. Invite students to tell stories, recreate incidents, copy significant passages from former writing, and quote people they interview. Final products should be personal narratives that reveal who they are as writers, and how and why they came to be the writers they are. Encourage creativity.

Show and Tell

During the class in which the papers are due, ask students to participate in an old-fashioned version of "show and tell." Have them sit in a circle and participate in a read-around activity in which each student reads his or her paper aloud and displays or passes around his or her writing relics. No one is to respond to the writing or the relics during the read-around session. Rather, students should write response notes to the reader.

Verbal Response

Once every person has presented his or her social history of writing, open the floor for response and discussion. The discussion will focus on answering the question, "How do social and political factors influence writer identity?"

A Move From History to Practice

In an effort to tie the social and political history of writing papers to pedagogy, tell students the following: "Based on what you have read, listened to, and discussed in class today, list 10 principles for teaching writing." Discuss these principles and attempt to synthesize them into a master list.

Summary

Writing a personal social history of writing can be a powerful assignment for students of all ages. This assignment would be ideal to assign at the beginning of the school year for several reasons. First, the prewriting conversations will help students begin to develop a vocabulary for talking about language and writing. Second, by having students brainstorm ideas about their writing histories and their successes and failures with writing, you will gain a great deal of insight into the types of writing your students prefer, how they want their writing to be read and graded, and ways that you can empower them; ultimately this information will assist you in planning effective instruction. If you ask your students to create 10 principles of how they believe writing should be taught, students will feel more invested in the process of learning to write. Third, by sharing their writing histories and writing relics, students will begin to know their peers on a deeper level, which is necessary for creating a comfortable, safe learning community. Fourth, when you participate in this project by writing with your students, you will develop your own principles for good writing instruction and will be able to synthesize your students' principles and needs.

Of course, some procedures in the activity can be adapted. Specifically, you will want to explore fully with students what it means to research and how one would conduct research on himself or herself. You also may need to revise the directions and create more structure for the process, depending on your students' abilities. In addition, you need to think about how you want to assess the students' progress and final products.

Assessment

It is nearly impossible to place a number or a letter grade on a project like this because the content is so personal. Therefore, you may not want to assess this piece of writing in any traditional sense, though

marginal and general responses related to the content of the history might be useful. Encourage students to include this assignment in their portfolios.

Enrichment

One way to enrich this project is to have students revisit their projects and 10 principles after they have read and discussed some theory and research about writing and the teaching of writing. The goal is to discover if student experiences connected in any way to the literature about teaching writing. Students could write a follow-up comparison-contrast paper or create a visual that represents these connections. Perhaps the most exciting prospect about developing one's personal history of writing is the possibility of obtaining some genuine insight into the person's relationship with the written word.

References

Brodkey, L. (1996). *Writing permitted in designated areas only*. Minneapolis, MN: University of Minnesota Press.

Seidman, I. (1998). *Interviewing as qualitative research: A guide for researchers in education and the social sciences* (2nd ed.). New York: Teachers College Press.

HISTORY OF MY WRITING STUDENT SAMPLE

"ME, WRITER"

I have never, as far as I can remember, viewed writing as a struggle. It has always been just the opposite—a liberating experience for me; a way of adding texture and layers to my thoughts and myself; a way of becoming something more through the words I place on paper. One reason I feel this sense of liberation though writing is that often times, in situations in which I am not entirely comfortable, my speaking stutters and stalls and my mind goes blank. In times like these, I rush to paper to convey what I really mean or meant to say. Other times, I turn to writing in order to figure things out in the first place, or even, more basically, to figure me out. I am fascinated by a tension I see in my writing between the manifestation of thoughts I already have, the discovery of buried ones, and the creation of new ones. Three very different actions seem to work together and against one another in the making of me and my sense of self and my impression on others, and I tend to pay close attention to this play.

There are three experiences that stand out in my mind, kind of as retrospective signposts, which brought me to this way in which I experience writing. They overlap and inform each other, and are, of course, informed by much that I won't have space to include in this short piece. I begin with my early college years, for this is when I became aware of myself as a writer and not just as a student writing for teachers. It was in my freshman year writing course where I found a voice, a place from which I felt comfortable enough to speak from, both outwardly and inwardly. My instructor gave us a lot of freedom and encouragement to write whatever it was we were compelled to. I found I wrote quite a bit about my relationship with my twin brother. It was enlightening and therapeutic—for the first time I sat back and contemplated and reflected about our problems and difficulties with one another. Among other things, I discovered my own heretofore unadmittable complicity in helping fuel our not getting along at the time. I sent my brother what I wrote and that was the beginning of our reconciliation. Writing worked something for me there; it enacted a change; it had some powers I was just becoming aware of and learning to use.

Another writing realization for me happened in a class called "Religion Through Western Literature." Through weekly journal responses to the theological novels we read, we were, again, encouraged to be as free and honest as possible, and to respond not from an analytical standpoint but more from an experiential place. Sculptors were encouraged to sculpt a response, and painters to paint one. Because of the nature of the readings, my prose responses took on the glean of a spiritual quest of sorts. They went deeper and more intimately into my own self and to my world than I had yet been. The time I spent on them too was like nothing I had experienced before. Relative

(continued)

HISTORY OF MY WRITING STUDENT SAMPLE (continued)

to my life, and especially in comparison to my business classes at the time, they were profound hours. The final assignment was to write about our "journey" through the semester, to connect or disconnect the various paths we had walked along. It really was a journey for me, and I realized I never would have come close to making that trip—let alone having the chance to continuously pack and unpack my bags—if it wasn't for the writing I did.

The third experience I am thinking of began about five years ago when I thankfully got into the letter writing habit with family and friends. This process fascinated me, that is, how I managed to turn rather ordinary stories into extra-ordinary ones. I learned a lot about how fiction and nonfiction merge and are really the same thing. The truth of some happening or event or feeling (at least for me) became not necessarily contingent, I learned, on strict adherence to the facts but rather on the essence of some feltness. For example, one morning I wrote a long letter to my parents from India about my experience eating breakfast in a hill town in Madya Pradesh. I described the food which was true, and the atmosphere, and the Sikh waiters, and the recently caught owl that was tethered to a tree on the back patio, but then I began to get creative about what was passing before the front door of the restaurant. Only half the time did what I put down actually walk past my eyes. The rest was made-up, but, and this is my point, it was still true to my experience there in that town and in India in general. The additions of the fictions better conveyed what I felt and was experiencing there. Those created images have since become more real than ever, as I have trouble now discerning what did pass by that door and what didn't. But it doesn't matter now; it never did.

To sum my learning from these three experiences, all of which were processes within themselves: I learned to trust my voice and first sensations; I learned that my writing has potential power and can effect change through its affect on me and on those close to me; I learned that writing can bring me places that the nebulousness of thinking or speaking alone cannot, to places I want to go to and even to places I don't yet know exist; I learned that the factuality, if you will, of what I write has little bearing on truth; and, most important, I learned that writing brings me great joy and a strong sense of feeling alive.

I play with all this in my journal. I use it as a tool to lift my spirits when I need to, or to record events when I have the feeling I've done something new or exciting or well or poorly. I use it to prove to me when I forget that, as is written in large letters on the first page, "I am an accumulation of thoughts, feelings, and gestures." When that accumulation of thoughts becomes static, it is to the pages of my journal I go to render them or to squeeze some life out of them. Then I see that I am not nothing.

We have to recognize imagination as a form of knowledge or our speculative fiction would vanish. Writers invent people they've never met, events that never happened, and countries that never existed. But if your fiction is to live, something deeply immediate and personal must be at its heart.

Stern, J. (1991). *Making shapely fiction* (p. 62). New York: Norton.

CREATIVE WRITING

IT'S BEEN TOO LONG SINCE YOU'VE GIVEN A CREATIVE WRITING ASSIGNMENT. It seems that every time you begin to plan something you panic and find yourself teaching something else. It has become frustrating for both you and your students. Time moves on and you have not covered half the material you had set out to and have not had the fun in the classroom you had promised yourself this year.

Activity	Entry point	Students work on	Preparation time needed
Creating Man	Creating a character	Characterization	Minimal
The Poe of Allegiance	Oral reading of Poe's "The Bells"	Style, satire	Minimal
Formatting the Story	Short story	Plot development	Substantial
Imaging Metaphors	Images	Imagery and symbolism	Substantial
Mystery Bags	Clip from Sherlock Holmes movie	Building suspense	Substantial

Your literature text has some decent short stories in it, and with any luck you might be able to create a few short assignments from one of them. Still you will have to spend most of your time discussing the elements of the short story, as well as having students read aloud. You thumb through the text, noting which stories exemplify setting and which stories best show characterization. You look over the inevitable questions at the end of the story. Nothing too new or exciting, but still, there are some possibilities.

As you place the textbook flat on you desk, you smile, remembering a short story you wrote as an assignment in college. You had been proud of it. Your central character had actually been an exaggerated version of your college roommate. She'd read the story and laughed out loud, never suspecting that she had provided the inspiration for the character. You decide that maybe it's time to break with tradition and address this year's short story unit from a much more creative angle.

The bell rings and students shuffle to their seats. Many open their textbooks and stare at you, waiting for the page number. You smile warmly at the class and mumble, "No textbooks today."

With these few words, you have momentarily engaged your students. You had almost forgotten what it felt like to have the attention of the entire class. "Everybody get out a sheet of paper and something to write with," you say. You turn to the chalkboard and write in big letters: As the rain began to fall, a scream was heard in the distance.

Anthony Kunkel

Creating Man: A Formula for Character

Type of activity: Individual. Approximate time: One 50-minute class period.

Objective

Students will learn how to create fictional characters, develop creative writing skills, and understand character development in writing.

Materials

Chalkboard or overhead needed for modeling.

Set-Up

None needed.

Procedure

This activity is best done in two parts—first the creation of a character, then the description. Instruct all students that they will be creating a character and that they will need a piece of paper and something to write with. *Note: With each part of this lesson, I will give an example in italics, and at the end of the explanation, I will provide the complete formula with the examples next to it. You will need to model an example for the students with each step of the instructions, one sentence at a time.*

First, instruct students to use their imagination and invent a character by giving it a first name and a last name. Then, using one sentence only, they are to write their character's full name on the paper and follow it with a sentence in which their character does something that shows action. *Jane Doe took hold of the chainsaw.*

Second, they are to give their character a thought. Have students add the following sentence to their first one: (fill in the blank)   , he/she thought. *I wonder how messy this will be, she thought.*

Next, instruct students to add one more sentence that begins with a pronoun and shows their character in active action (as opposed to passive action). *She opened the door softly and stepped quietly into the room.*

Now tell students to add one more sentence, giving their characters a memory or thought about the past. *She thought of her last husband and a time when her life had been much simpler.*

Finally, have students write one more sentence that shows action and concludes the scene they have written thus far. *Jane moved quietly to the edge of the bed where the man lay sleeping, then smiling coldly, she pulled the cord and brought the saw to life.*

FORMULA	EXAMPLE
1. (full name) and action sentence.	Jane Doe took hold of the chainsaw.
2. (fill in the blank) , he/she thought.	I wonder how messy this will be, she thought.
3. Pronoun and active action sentence.	She opened the door softly and stepped quietly into the room.
4. Memory or thought about the past.	She thought of her last husband and a time when her life had been much simpler.
5. Action sentence that concludes the scene.	Jane moved quietly to the edge of he bed where the man lay sleeping, then smiling coldly, she pulled the cord and brought the saw to life.

Once all students have concluded their character scenes, begin the description formula for their characters. This part of the activity will focus on giving physical description through action to their newly invented characters. To help avoid confusion it is best to inform students that the descriptions they are about to write have nothing to do with the scenes they have just created, except for the fact that they are using the same character—same character, different scene.

First, have students write their character's full name followed by "stood in front of the mirror." This will be the first sentence of the description. *Jane Doe stood in front of the mirror.*

Then, instruct students to follow the first sentence with one descriptive sentence about their character; it is helpful to explain to the class that their characters are now looking at themselves in the mirror and should notice something that helps describe them. *The wrinkles around her eyes seemed deeper then she remembered.*

Third, tell students to begin the next sentence of their description with the proper pronoun for their character, and finish it with some descriptive action— have their character do something that will tell something about their looks. *She lifted a trembling hand to her short dark hair.*

Next, have students give their character a thought using only one sentence: __(fill in the blank)__, he/she thought. *Where has the time gone, she thought.*

Last, students should write one action sentence in which their character either leaves the mirror or breaks it. *She lowered her hand, shook her head sadly, and walked away from the mirror.*

FORMULA	EXAMPLE
1. __(full name)__ standing in front of mirror.	Jane Doe stood in front of the mirror.
2. A physically descriptive sentence.	The wrinkles around her eyes seemed deeper then she remembered.
3. Pronoun and descriptive sentence.	She lifted a trembling hand to her short dark hair.
4. __(fill in the blank)__, he/she thought.	Where has the time gone, she thought.
5. Concluding action and leave mirror.	She lowered her hand, shook her head sadly, and walked away from the mirror.

Summary

This lesson has had remarkable success in all of my classes. If possible, I recommend you read these character sentences aloud and talk about the depth created with the description and thoughts of the characters. The formula, if followed, will always read well, and the students will enjoy hearing the quality they have produced. The step-by-step, sentence-by-sentence approach to creating a character is one that even the most reluctant of students will pick up easily, and the quality of the characters many of them create will surprise and engage them. What I find generally happens in my class is that many of the students will realize that they have created a short piece of quality fiction they did not realize they were capable of writing, and this realization leads to a willing class full of engaged students.

Enrichment

An idea that works well in conjunction with Creating Man is following the activity with a short-story assignment. I ask students to write short stories, using the characters they have created in these sentences. This, I have found, will increase the quality of the stories that are written and will make them much more personal to the students who are writing them.

Gregory Stanley

The Poe of Allegiance

Type of activity: Individual.
Approximate time: 30 minutes.

Objective

Students will recreate the U.S. "Pledge of Allegiance" using a different writing style, in this case, that of Edgar Allan Poe.

Materials

Pen and paper or a computer with a word processing program.

Set-Up

Students will read a number of famous literary pieces that have a very definite style. One of my favorites is Edgar Allan Poe's "The Bells."

Discuss the style of the author, including meter, rhyme scheme, imagery, and repetition.

Procedure

Tell the students, "You are Edgar Allan Poe and have just finished composing your last poem, 'The Bells.' Using the same basic writing style, rewrite 'The Pledge of Allegiance.'" Once they are done writing, have students read their work aloud.

Summary

The Poe of Allegiance is a great exercise to teach students exactly what constitutes a writer's style. You can talk to students about it for hours, but this activity makes it more personal. The Poe of Allegiance gives students the opportunity to be creative while giving them a supporting scaffold on which to work.

Enrichment

Other similar exercises:

"You are Mickey Spillane and have just finished writing *Kiss Me Deadly*. Rewrite Dr. Seuss's *Green Eggs and Ham*."

"You are Dr. Seuss. Rewrite the preamble to the U.S. Constitution."

THE POE OF ALLEGIANCE STUDENT SAMPLE

I pledge allegience to the flag,
Our nation's flag
The gallant flag
the flag, the flag, the flag.
To its stars
and its red bars
that burn into my soul.
stars, stars, stars,
red bars, red bars, red bars.
I pledge allegience to the flag

I pledge allegience to the flag
One nation
Unique in all creation.
Under God as a foundation.
I pledge allegience to the flag,
flag, flag, flag, flag, flag, flag, flag.
I pledge allegience to the flag.

Anthony Kunkel

Formatting the Story: Focusing on Setting, Character, and Plot

**Type of activity: Group.
Approximate time: Five class
periods.**

Objective

Students will learn to identify and discuss setting, character, and plot within a short story; will demonstrate descriptive and creative writing techniques; will demonstrate rewording and revision skills; will create characters for fictional writing; and will write plot and setting treatments for short stories.

Materials

Creative pictures or paintings will be needed, one for each group or individual, as the case may be. In the past I have used various covers from *The New Yorker* or other magazines, always with the titles cut off. Art transparencies will also work. Basically, you will need a colorful visual that can stimulate a large number of stories from the students.

Set-Up

None needed.

Procedure

Day One

Select a short story that can be read in one class period with time left for a short discussion. The story is intended primarily as a means to demonstrate setting, character, and plot. Once the story is read, hold a short discussion of its setting, character(s), and plot, focusing specifically on what these elements of story are, and any piece of the story that may have exemplified them well. It is opportune to introduce conflict and resolution during an explanation of plot. I have made it a habit of telling my students that plot in a short story is "the sequence of events and the conflict and resolution that take place within a story."

Day Two

After a short recap of setting, character, and plot, divide students into small groups, and hand out the creative pictures in a random order. To make the activity fun, put the pictures in a paper bag and have a member from each group reach in and pull one out. Groups are then instructed to look at their picture and discuss the story that is inside it. Instruct them to think in terms of setting, character, and plot, and decide where and when the story takes place, who the main character of the story is, and the story's plot. Also, groups should discuss the conflict of the story and how it will be resolved. At this point, refer to the story read the previous day and again briefly discuss its setting, characters, and plot. Once the groups have settled in and have begun developing some ideas (typically about 10 minutes), give them the instructional handout on page 103.

Once all groups have had a chance to go over the handouts and all questions regarding the assignment have been answered, it is time to get to work. Require that once groups start writing, every group member has a chance to write. How the groups split up the work is up to them, but all members must do equal writing. *Note: It helps to give students daily expectations and deadlines to ensure they stay on task and don't waste time. For this assignment it is normal*

FORMAT YOUR STORY

Your group's assignment is to turn your picture into a format for the world's most creative short story. You are required to discuss your picture as a group and to share your ideas. You will be creating the setting, the main character, and the plot of the story your picture tells. You will not be writing this story, but instead focusing intently on the three elements mentioned. Imagination and creative writing will be required, and nothing less than brilliance will be accepted. In order to provide the best possible format for your story, please follow these directions:

1. Write at least one page describing the setting of your story. Focus only on the setting and be as creative and visual as possible in your writing. (For example, "The grass rippled softly in the breeze, an ocean of green shimmering on the surface. The sky above was endless, clear and blue, with slight tinges of orange creeping just across the horizon…") The best way to determine everything about your setting is for you to imagine you are there, standing and looking around. What do you see, smell, and hear? What is the weather like? Think of as many details as possible and paint a picture with words that will put the reader at that place and time. Please be careful not to go into plot when describing—give only description, not what's going on.

2. Write at least one page describing the main character of your story. If your picture has no characters, you will need to invent one to go with your story. Focus on one main character for your story and write everything there is to know about your character. Leave the plot of the story out of your character description, and instead give your character a history on paper. Discuss among your group when your character was born (or created), where he was born, what his childhood was like, what his parents (or creator) were like, any events that shaped the way he is today, what he likes to eat, music preferences if any, odd habits he may have, clothes he likes to wear, and anything else you want the reader to know. Be sure to include a good physical description of your character.

3. Write at least one page telling the plot of your story. Now is when you describe what your story is about. Please do not attempt to write the story, but instead give a summary of the sequence of events within the story. Also, with your plot summary include an explanation of the conflict that will take place in the story and how it will be resolved. On your plot summary, be creative and clever as possible. This is a good opportunity to show off your group's imagination. If your group finds it hard to summarize the plot and conflict with only a page of writing, you probably have some creative ideas that need more explanation—this is good.

for much of the explanation and set-up to take a good portion of the class, so I ask that each group only begin their writing, and have something to show by the end of the period. Also, because this is an in-class assignment, all groups should leave their format work in the classroom, along with their pictures and the instructional handout.

Day Three

Hand out the formats-in-progress to their respective groups and allow students to commence work. This is a good day to monitor their progress and assist any student who is struggling with the intensity of the writing assignment. Typically on this day you should require all groups to have completed their formats. These are actually only rough drafts, so allow them to sacrifice spelling, punctuation, and neatness in order to complete the formats within the time frame allowed. For the faster groups that tend to finish too early, you can allow them to read a short story, or you could go over weaknesses in their formats that they may wish to spend some time on. Encourage students to use a thesaurus while they write. *Once again, it is best to collect all work before the students leave.*

Day Four

This is revision day. Most groups should have completed their formats by now, but those who may be lagging behind will have a chance to catch up to-

day. Hand out the format drafts to the groups and instruct each group to separate the setting, character, and plot, and then to divide the elements among their group. Instruct students to make sure they have a paper in front of them other than the one that they did all (or most) of the writing on. Once all students have their assigned formats, they are instructed to do a complete revision on the paper they have in front of them. Changes, rewording, adding synonyms, deleting, adding description, spelling, and grammar checks should be mandatory (I instruct those students who are not sure of what's expected, that for every three sentences written they should make changes or additions to at least one sentence). Once group members have completed their revision, they are to pass it to the left (within their group) and repeat the process on the paper that's being passed to them. All group members will do a complete revision on all pages written within their groups thus far, including their own. *Note: It is effective in this part of the activity for you to actually sit down with some of the groups and join the revision process. I often sit with a group and rewrite a sentence or two of theirs, usually using some colorful adjectives. This helps some of the students see firsthand exactly what is expected in their revision.*

Day Five

Give students the entire class period to finish revising and to write polished copies of their formats. All revisions from the previous day should be included on their final copies, and all spelling and grammar errors should be corrected. The final product should be written neatly, with each member of the group doing his or her part in the rewriting of the final copy. Instruct students to give their final formats a title and include a title page—the more colorful the better. (I usually require rough drafts to be turned in with final copies and include the revision done on them in the grading process.)

Summary

Some of my students' best descriptive writing has been produced during this activity, and most of my students finish this lesson knowing more about the short story than they would have with any amount of book work. Within a group activity, the students become easily motivated and often can be seen together agonizing and arguing over different ways to best word a particular phrase or description. This is cooperative learning at its best. Although I did not mention oral presentations in the lesson, it is not uncommon for many of the groups to ask for the opportunity to show their ideas. If time permits, I always try to accommodate them.

Enrichment

Once all the formats are done, there are several things that can be done with them. One idea that has worked well in my classes is to redistribute the formats, making sure no group has its own, and have the groups write the actual short story. This creates a good lesson on perception and communication in writing, and really sends a message to the students on how effective and necessary good description can be in their writing.

Anthony Kunkel

Imaging Metaphors

Type of activity: Group or individual.

Approximate time: 50 minutes.

Objective

Students will discuss the use of images as vehicles for symbolic and metaphorical writing, learn creative writing techniques, and use images in their writing to create symbolism and metaphors.

Materials

Index cards or slips of paper with selected images written on them (an example of suggested images is provided with this lesson).

Set-Up

Class should be divided into groups of two or three, unless the activity is being assigned individually.

Procedure

Step One

Introduce the activity with a short discussion on imagery in writing and on how various images can be used in writing to create symbolism and metaphors, eliciting and giving examples when possible.

Step Two

Each group (or individual) is to be given an index card containing one written image. Once all groups have received their cards, they are instructed to discuss the image that they have been given, and create a short piece of writing of approximately one page, using their image as symbolically as possible. This image is to become the central metaphor of whatever it is that they are writing. Students may write an essay, a short piece of fiction, or a poem—the only requirement is that the writing must be as metaphorical as possible.

Step Three

Once all groups have finished creating metaphors from their images, oral presentations will ensue. Each group should explain what their image was intended to represent, and how they chose to make it so.

Listed below are some suggested images that may prove effective:

A rusty swing set

An abandoned factory

An abandoned garden

A single rose

A broken doll

A sudden thunderstorm

Summary

Students enjoy Imaging Metaphors and will produce some wonderful writing and discussion. I created this lesson as a prereading activity for the Crossing Edson's Bridge activity (see page 141), but have found it to be useful as a prepoetry activity as well.

Enrichment

Using this lesson prior to Crossing Edson's Bridge is a great set-up for a unit on reading comprehension and figurative language within selected readings.

CREATIVE WRITING

Coleen Baines and Lawrence Baines

Mystery Bags

Type of activity: Group.
Approximate time: Works best over 2 days.

Objective

Students will learn how to construct suspense effectively and will gain an appreciation of the genre of detective fiction.

Materials

Divide your class into groups of three or four students.

Have as many bags for clues as you need (six to eight bags for a class of 24 students).

Set-Up

Show students an excerpt from a film depicting the adventures of Sherlock Holmes in which Holmes and Watson attempt to deduce the significance of certain clues.

Have students read Sir Arthur Conan Doyle's *The Blue Carbuncle* or *Hound of the Baskervilles*, or John Mortimer's *Rumpole a la Carte*, or a short story by Raymond Chandler. (See the Resources appendix that begins on page 167 for full citations of these works.) Discuss with students the techniques that authors use to build suspense and how sleuths use their powers of deduction to solve crimes.

Gather together objects that might be found at the scene of a crime—a note, a pair of scissors, a ticket stub, a key, a bottle, etc. Try to put 6 to 14 unique objects in each bag.

Procedure

Discuss how Sherlock Holmes (or the detective from the film clip and novels you used) solved crimes.

Tell students that a crime has been committed and that they must use their powers of deduction in

MYSTERY BAGS STUDENT SAMPLE

An umbrella, still wet with the late night icy drops, is in a puddle near the door. On the table lies the rough draft of an article, face-up, still paper-clipped with a few stray pencil marks of indecision in the margins. The deceased preferred to edit with a pencil.

Her limp body was still warm with no signs of a physical struggle or any evident wound. No liquid around the desk, no bottle of wine, no sign of poison. A torn ticket stub to a movie theater on the East Side was on the floor near her foot.

Jumbo enters the scene in his trademark moth-eaten old football letter jacket, and he picks up the torn ticket stub. The digital clock has been knocked to the ground and is blinking an infinite repetition of 2:52. Flashing, flashing…too easy.

Jumbo's wet hair, plaid shirt, and three-day growth of whiskers make him look as if he might be one of the homeless along Washington Avenue, but the uniforms on duty stay out of his way as he wanders about the room. He plays with a rubber band with his fingers and wears a pencil behind his left ear. He looks down at the table and picks up an envelope that had been torn carefully down the side. Opening the letter, he reads the first sentence: "Congratulations! Your article on human rights in China has been accepted for publication in *International Trade Quarterly*…" Next to the letter is an empty disk case, but no sign of a disk.

order to piece the clues together. From the available evidence, every group should decide these facts:

- The crime
- The victim
- The perpetrator
- The sleuth (must have a name, some readily apparent physical features, and distinctive tastes)
- Obstacles to solving the crime

From this, students should write collaboratively within their groups a mystery story that uses these components.

Summary

Mystery Bags enlivens the study of detective fiction. Especially for those who seem to have some difficulty getting started, Mystery Bags effectively promotes students' storytelling potential.

Enrichment

An obvious next step is for students to perform, audiotape, or videotape their stories.

Point of view is the most complex element of fiction. Although it lends itself to analysis, definitions, and diagrams, it is finally a question of relationship among writer, characters, and reader—subject like any relationship to organic subtleties.... Rather than thinking of point of view as an opinion or belief, begin with the more literal synonym of "vantage point."

Burroway, J. (1987). *Writing fiction* (p. 223). Boston, MA: Little, Brown.

POINT OF VIEW AND TONE

AS SHELDON, AN INTELLIGENT YOUNG MAN IN YOUR FOURTH-PERIOD ENGLISH CLASS, finishes Ransom's "Bells for John Whiteside's Daughter," you look around the class for any sign of understanding or emotion. Most students continue looking at the textbook, certain that if they don't make eye contact with you that they won't get called on.

"Who can tell me what the tone of this poem is?" You wait. A few students look nervously at you and one young lady tentatively raises her hand.

"Confusion?"

You smile to yourself. Of course it would be an answer that doesn't tell you if she really understands Ransom's poem or not. The poem is confusing, possesses a certain complexity of tone, but her answer is not conclusive enough. As the silence drags on, you become uncomfortable. Tim, the quiet boy in back who usually comes up with a response when no one else can, is going to great lengths to appear distracted. His pencil has fallen under his desk and continues to elude his reaching fingers—Tim's way of communicating that the answers are not in him at the moment. You had done "The Raven" earlier this year and the responses had been much more enthusiastic. Even your low-level tech prep class had discovered in Poe's words a sense of rhythm strong enough to produce a rap of surprising quality. You had been surprised when Cedric first stood up and began beating out a rhythm, but even more surprised when Titus put Poe's words to it. Something about Poe had connected with students, and for a while it had appeared that students understood. Unfortunately, their understanding was fleeting. Perhaps your students need to take a more active role in understanding the subtleties of tone and point of view.

Activity	Entry point	Students work on	Preparation time needed
Someone Else's Shoes	Oral reading of Mark Twain's "A Dog's Tale"	Point of view	Minimal
Tombstone Fiction	Field trip to a cemetery	Point of view, research	Substantial
Moody House	Guided imagery	Mood	Minimal
Tabloid Exposé	*National Enquirer*-type tabloids	Tone and purpose	Substantial
Secrets	O'Henry's "Gift of the Magi"	Subtlety and tone	Substantial

Alan Perry

Someone Else's Shoes

**Type of activity: Individual.
Approximate time: 1 to 2 days.**

Objective

Students will create a story from a different point of view, thus enhancing creativity.

Materials

A set of abridged and adapted copies of Mark Twain's story "A Dog's Tale" for each class member.

Set-Up

Give each student a copy of "A Dog's Tale" to read.

Procedure

In "A Dog's Tale," Mark Twain tells a story from the point of view of an animal. Have students imagine that they are either an animal or an inanimate object, and ask them to write a story about something that happens to them. Here are some suggestions for objects, but don't limit the students to this list:

leaf in autumn on a cool, breezy day

mannequin on display at a department store

hamburger in a fast-food restaurant

fish in an aquarium

mirror in a teenager's bedroom

chocolate chip about to be made into a cookie

garbage bag in the kitchen

abused and neglected literature textbook

groundhog on Groundhog's Day

pothole on the highway

automated banking machine with a nasty sense of humor

pumpkin on the day after Halloween

"peach fuzz" about to be shaved off an adolescent male's face for the first time

proud, new pimple on the otherwise clear complexion of a self-conscious student

first snowflake of winter, on a quiet night

baseball in the hands of a pitcher

day-old doughnut that nobody seems to want

Venus' fly trap tempting a hungry fly

caterpillar preparing for winter

football on the night of the homecoming game

annoying fly or mosquito harassing a person and enjoying it

Christmas ornament after New Year's Day

Summary

Students will gain empathy and insight by writing from different perspective than their own.

Enrichment

After students have completed their first story, you can have them write two more stories from two other related perspectives. For instance, if a student wrote her first story about a fly that is harassing someone, she could then write two more stories from the point of view of two of the following suggestions:

the person whom the fly is bothering

the sandwich that the person is holding that the fly keeps landing on

a bystander who is amused by watching the person swat the fly

a scientist who specializes in flies that is observing this scene

Again, suggest possible points of view for the students to use if they need help, but allow them the opportunity to develop and use their own ideas.

Blake Tenore

Tombstone Fiction

**Type of activity: Individual.
Approximate time: One to two
class periods.**

Objective

Students will write from a perspective other than their own, explore interest across the curriculum, and engage in an imaginative and creative writing activity to create a persona.

Materials

Access to a cemetery is ideal for this activity, but creating fictional or nonfictional headstones with information such as dates of birth and death, city of residence, and a notable accomplishment can be just as effective.

Set-Up

If unable to take a field trip to a cemetery, all students need to be provided with a tombstone that lists enough information to make assumptions. It is recommended that tombstones be provided with varied information such as age spans, living during specific historical events, notable accomplishments, or memorable captions.

Procedure

Both of the following options are designed to follow a lesson or discussion of point of view and perspective as it pertains to reading and writing.

Option One

Take students on a walking field trip to a nearby cemetery and give them a few minutes to tour the grounds, read tombstones, and simply get used to being in a cemetery (for some it may be their first time). Have them choose one grave to write about; they should choose one that for some reason appeals to them—one in which they take a special interest. Allow them to spend a few moments studying, pondering the name, dates, events of the person's life. (When I did this with my classes, many students were deeply moved by what they saw and were determined to do

fictional justice to the life of the deceased.) After they have copied the information from the stones, have students jot some initial thoughts about the person's life.

Either for homework or in class the next day, instruct students to write a first-person narrative from the perspective of the deceased as if he or she was speaking to the student. The narrative may include childhood memories, significant events of adult life, child rearing, and events surrounding death. Encourage students to be as detailed and imaginative as possible in their narratives, reminding them that these are elements that bring fiction to life.

Option Two

In case a cemetery is not available, prepare suitable "tombstones" from which students can choose. Allow students to choose their own stones; of course, a "connection" like one felt from being in a cemetery is difficult, but something about a particular stone still may appeal to individuals. Then follow procedures from Option One.

Time should be left for students to share their work.

Summary

This exercise opens doors for young writers as they begin to experiment with points of view other than their own. Not only will it broaden their repertoire as writers, but it also forces them to see a piece of history from someone else's perspective. If possible, this may be a valuable exercise to use in a cross-curricular project with social studies or history classes.

Enrichment

Have students create and write biographical sketches of characters from objects such as a wallet, a purse, old jewelry, or other personal artifacts.

Assessment

As with all creative and imaginative writing, this activity is difficult to evaluate with a grade. One option is to have students write a process memo describing the decisions they made as they created this fictional piece; from this you should be able to tell to what extent the writer wrestled with ideas and how carefully he or she has formulated thoughts. Another option is to workshop these pieces in class by putting students into groups for peer responses.

TOMBSTONE FICTION STUDENT SAMPLE

Frederick Ray Jenkins
October 17, 1982–March 22, 1998

This is the story of my very short, tragic life. I was too young to die, I had so many things I wanted to do with my life. Up until I was sixteen years old, I had a great life.

I grew up in a little town in Virginia. We lived not to far from the coast. Everyone in the town knew each other, we had all grown up together. I had a great family. My mom and dad were still together after twenty-four great years. I had two sisters, twelve and fourteen. My life was practically perfect. I made good grades and I was on the varsity football team as quarterback.

Anyway, to get to what happened to me that cost me my life. I had just started my junior year in high school. I had been dating this girl since my freshman year. She was the love of my life. I really thought she was the one I wanted to be with for the rest of my life. Well, the second week of school she totally dumped me for another guy. To make things worse, it was one of my best friends. I was so depressed. My grades dropped tremendously, and I was about to get kicked off the team because of my grades. But I just didn't seem to care. My parents were very worried about me. They tried to talk to me, but I didn't care.

My birthday finally came around and I had just gotten my driver's license. It had been three months since she left me. One of my friends was having this big party at his house because his parents were gone for the weekend. I didn't know if I wanted to go because I figured my ex-girlfriend would be there with my ex-best friend. I decided to go. I noticed them the first thing. I was depressed so when they brought the beer in, I got one. I started drinking a lot. Beer after beer, and I just kept drinking.

Every time I looked over at them, it just made me want to drink more. Finally, the party ended and I was about to go home. My friend tried to get me to stay the night because I was so drunk, but I didn't listen. I got in my car and headed home. All of a sudden, I swerved off the road and crashed into a telephone pole. I knew my life was over because of a dumb decision I made. The crash killed me instantly.

So, you see, I died because of that dumb decision. I caused my parents and sisters a lot of heartache and grief because I chose to drink and drive. I wish I could go back and start over because I would have made the right decision and stayed over at my friend's house. Maybe then I'd have my life back.

Anthony Kunkel

The Moody House: A Perspective Lesson for Creative Description

**Type of activity: Individual.
Approximate time: One to two
class periods.**

*Note: This activity was adapted from several exercises in John
Gardner's book,* The Art of Fiction. *(1985). New York: Vintage Press.*

Objective

Students will learn to write from a variety of perspectives, demonstrate creative writing techniques, and incorporate the use of mood as a descriptive vehicle for writing.

Materials

None needed.

Set-Up

None needed.

Procedure

First and foremost, the students will need to use their imaginations for this exercise. Instruct all students to imagine that they are standing on the side of a road staring at an old abandoned house; it may be useful for some students to close their eyes for a moment and attempt to form a picture of the house in their mind. Once they have done this, give all students the following perspective to write from:

> You are happily married with two children. This morning you received news that your family has just been killed in a terrible plane crash. You are now devastated with loss. Your world has collapsed and you feel empty, sad, and lost.

Ask students to write at least a half page from this perspective and describe the house they have just imagined. The idea is for each student to describe only the house, capturing the perspective character's sadness and sense of loss in that description. At no time should the student use the first person "I" in their description, or tell any of the details about the perspective character. The student should describe the house only, and in that description capture the feelings and emotions of the perspective from which they are writing. What works well with this lesson is to read a sample from either a student who did well on this assignment, or create a sample that models what is expected.

The second part of this activity is the same as the first, only you will ask students to open their minds and write from another perspective. Inform students that they are standing in the same spot on the same road looking at the same house on the same day. This time, though, they are looking at the house from a different perspective:

> You have just gotten engaged. Your boss found out and gave you the promotion that you have been waiting for. You're excited about the future, you're happy, you're in love, and you've never been more at peace with the world or had such a feeling of hope for the future.

Once again, instruct the students to describe that same house, only now their descriptions are to reflect how happy and full of hope their perspective character is. Also, once again, they should be instructed to leave all personal details out of their description and concentrate on only describing the house. At this point read another sample and give students an example of how to do this. I say, "For instance, a swing set that formerly lay toppled and discarded, a vision of loss and abandonment, now could create an image of laughter, a vision of children to come, laughing and playing, a promise of hope for the future."

The final part of this activity is more for fun than any real descriptive value, but most students will become excited to try this, and this in itself helps create an environment for further creativity. As they have done before, students should describe the same house, and again, they will write from a different perspective. This time students will write from the following perspective:

> You have just escaped from a mental institution. You are completely insane and view the world differently than a normal person would. Your world is demented, as are you.

As they have been required to do in the previous descriptions, students should leave all mention of personal details out of their descriptions. They only indication to the reader of how demented the character is will be in the description of the house.

Summary

This activity has been a turning point for many of the students in my class. Many students who make an effort on this activity will write something better and more creative than anything they have written before. The effectiveness of description through mood is a lesson that is learned well, and it is not uncommon for a student to come in the next day and talk about how they did this with their friends or family once they got home. I do make a point of reading some of the better descriptions out loud to the class, especially from those students who are very reluctant and tentative about their writing.

Enrichment

Follow this activity with another that is almost identical but personal to the students—make it relevant. Instruct students to think of something that happened in their lives that was important and then to remember where it happened. Students should also try to remember how they felt while it was happening and write that feeling in one word (*happy, sad, angry, frightened, excited*). Once this is done, instruct them to describe the setting of that moment, writing nothing about their personal feelings, but using descriptions of the setting to capture the emotion they felt. Follow this by reading aloud the descriptions and asking the class to guess the emotion that was being expressed.

Sydeana Martin

Tabloid Exposé

Type of activity: Individual, can be bridged to group.
Approximate time: One 50-minute class period.

Objective

Students will understand connections between reading and writing, will write for different purposes and audiences, and will use tone appropriately.

Materials

Handout of a short story, folk tale, or news article; pens and paper.

Set-Up

You may want to write some headlines on the board such as, "Two-Headed Man Says Elvis Is Alive" or "Michael Jackson Is an Alien." This will serve as a base for a discussion of tabloids and their audience, tone, and purpose.

Procedure

Explain to students that the class will be reading a folk tale about a young boy who experiences something rather strange. Each student should have his or her own copy of the story. (I use "The Forsaken Brother" as retold by Jane Johnsonston Schoolcraft, originally from the Chippewa Indians. I use this folk tale because it is very short and it also contains something of the fantastic—the little boy turns into a wolf by the end of the story.) Have students read the folk tale once silently, then read it aloud as a class. Ask students to generate some ideas for titles that they would see if this folk tale were to be reported in the *National Enquirer* or *The Globe*, such as: "Wolf-Boy Found in Local Woods," "Teen Wolf Lives," or "Help! My Brother Is a Wolf!" Next, ask students to pretend they are reporters for the *National Enquirer* and re-port the story of the "Forsaken Brother" as it would appear in a tabloid, keeping in mind audience, tone, and purpose.

Summary

I like this activity because it connects reading and writing, encourages students to be creative, and the students themselves see it as fun. I use it when we need a break from a longer unit or as a way of introducing a new unit such as folklore.

Enrichment

Although this activity can be used as an "ice-breaker" to a unit in a short 50-minute session, I have also used it to emphasize audience, tone, and purpose in longer works of literature. It is a good way to review what has happened so far in a novel or screenplay. You also could place students into small groups and have them peer edit one another's papers. This allows for the entire writing process to take place: planning, drafting, feedback by peers, and revising. Ask students to draw pictures for their tabloid article, and publish them in the room and in the school newspaper, which always brings other students to your door asking questions.

Lawrence Baines

Secrets

Type of activity: Individual. Approximate time: Two 50-minute periods of writing.

Objective

Students will indirectly describe a secret (or secrets) between two persons, using subtleties of dialogue, setting, and tone. This exercise is particularly useful in getting students to write with subtlety and wit.

Materials

Pen and paper or computer with word processor.

Set-Up

Have students read and discuss O. Henry's short story "The Gift of the Magi" (available at: http://www.night.net/christmas/Gift-Magi.html). Emphasize that O. Henry does not simply reveal what happens in the story, but that he allows the actions and dialogue of the characters to illuminate the secrets, the characters' fears, and each character's feelings about the other.

Prepare two sheets of paper with the following scenarios on them:

1. You have just been nominated for an internship as an artist-in-residence at *Le Louvre*. You are best friends with B, who has on more than one occasion come through for you. Recently, you have found that B has developed some severe problems with gambling. B has told you that some men have been looking for him lately to collect gambling debts he owes. You have repeatedly lectured B on his gambling, but you suspect that he continues to gamble away every cent he earns. You are uncertain what course to take about yourself and your relationship with B. You wonder if you should seize the opportunity to go on the art internship or to devote yourself to helping rehabilitate B during this critical time. Of course, B would not want you to forego a career opportunity just to help him. You need to find out if B is still gambling and how B might react to the possibility of you leaving the country.

2. You have just won $4 million in the state lottery. You wonder if you should tell A, who used to be your best friend, because he has been acting very strangely lately, and you do not understand why. A seems to have everything going for him. But A has repeatedly criticized you for gambling too much. True, you do spend way too much of your paycheck on silly longshots, but now your gambling has finally paid off. You are not sure if A still wants to be your friend or not, and you fear that revealing that you have just won $4 million will perhaps push him into being your friend, just because of the money. But you want a *real* friendship, not one based on money. A few weeks ago, your family decided to go to Ireland this summer for 3 weeks. You considered asking A to go with you and your family, but now you think that you would rather not invite A if he is going to act like your guard dog. You would still like to be A's friend, but you need some time to think about being a millionaire, too. In this conversation with A, you want to find out why he has been acting so strangely and if he really likes you for who you are. You have to decide today whether or not you want A to go to Ireland with you and your family. Perhaps it might be best simply not to mention the trip at all.

Procedure

Discuss "The Gift of the Magi."

Pick the two most theatrical students in class. Ask one student to read the scenario for A and another student to read the scenario for B. Then ask the two students to have an impromptu 5- to 10-minute conversation in front of the class.

Tell the class that they are about to witness a scene in which each of the characters has a secret that he or she is hiding from the other. Ask the class to note how the two characters interact—the dialogue, facial reactions, and gestures. Hand out the two scenarios to the two theatrical students and allow them to act it out. At the end of the skit, discuss the ways that silence and awkwardness can imply meaning. Have students guess at each character's secret, then have characters A and B reveal them.

Ask students to write a short dialogue between two persons, in which at least one has a secret. The idea is to make the writer write through implication and indirect description.

Summary

Although Secrets seems a bit complicated at first, some of the best writing I have ever received from students has been the result of this activity. Further, Secrets seems to help students understand the power of understatement and implication and seems to transfer somewhat to students' nonfictional writing.

Enrichment

Once students have written their stories, they form groups of three to four. Students read each story, decide which would make the best short play, and vote on it. Two students act out the scenario and the author directs. If a camcorder is available, the fourth student (or the author) films. If no camcorder is available, then the fourth student acts as critic. Eventually the story is turned in and the play is performed (or the film is shown).

Literature was written to make an impact. Readers must talk about the literature, argue about it, look for points of agreement and disagreement with the author, look for ways it connects to their lives. We must keep this at the heart of what we do in the literature class and find ways to value and evaluate the meaning our students make through literature.

Tchudi, S., & Mitchell, D. (1999). *Exploring and teaching the English language arts* (p. 236). New York: Longman.

LITERATURE

YOU DECIDED TO BECOME AN ENGLISH TEACHER ONLY AFTER YOU WORKED AT MANY OTHER JOBS—real estate salesperson, fry cook, retail manager, bartender, banker, and baker. You made more money in other fields, but you always wound up missing the books. As a teacher of English, you get paid to read and think. Not a lot of money, of course, but in no other profession would it be important to know why the caged bird sings, who Big Brother really is, and the significance of a scarlet A.

Activity	Entry point	Students work on	Preparation time needed
From Book to Poem	Recently read book	Poetry	Minimal
Evaluating Irony	Contemporary song	Effective use of irony	Substantial
Overcoming Adversities	Pearl Buck's *The Big Wave*, current events	Reading and performance	Substantial
Crossing Edson's Bridge	Short short story	Style	Minimal
Letter to Olaudan	Slave narrative	Historical perspective, format for letters	Substantial

But this year your students seem less motivated to read than ever. So you've made it a habit of perusing bookstores on a regular basis. You cruise for hours the "megastores" that are part of a national bookstore chain, intermittently sipping your coffee and exploring for books that might interest you or your students. At the neighborhood used-book store, you burrow for books amidst the live-in cats and discarded stacks of romance novels, all the time rationalizing that you can buy twice as many books as you ordinarily would because of the discounted price. If you use the Internet, you always wind up ordering books that you know you can't really afford from online bookstores. But you load up the charge card anyway.

In short, you are a book junkie. You have enough books at home in your "to-be-read" pile that it would be impossible to finish them all within a single lifetime. You want to share your love of books with your students and help instill in them a yearning to read and learn. But you won't be able to do that by simply asking them to open their books and begin reading. You need to get them interested first.

Mike Rychlik

From Book to Poem

Type of activity: Individual literary response.
Approximate time: Two class periods.

Objective

Students will respond creatively to preread text, will reflect insight and empathy for characters and setting, and will perform an original poetic work.

Materials

Novel and poetry model.

Set-Up

After reading a literary text, study in class a poetry model for students to use as an example for their own work.

Procedure

As a postreading prewriting activity, introduce a poet or style of poetry for the students to model. For instance, after my juniors read *Cannery Row* and *Catcher in the Rye*, we read the poetry of Walt Whitman and studied free verse.

After my freshmen read *Christmas Carol*, we read *Spoon River Anthology*, and the students wrote first-person eulogies in a mock Edgar Lee Masters style to explain how Scrooge would have been remembered had he died as he was depicted in Stave Four (Ghost of Future).

Instruct the class to write a poem based on an event or character in the book you have just finished reading. On the objectives you present to your class, clearly state that students must show empathy with the characters and their conflicts. They also must perform their poems in front of their classmates.

Summary

Too often, we the teachers become overly concerned with checking to make sure that our students have read and have comprehended a required text. Consequently, our follow-ups are all too often multiple-choice tests that measure if the students have fulfilled their obligations by reading the text, following the plot, understanding the conflicts, and regurgitating stock interpretations. I've discovered that when students write poetry in response to literature as an achievement activity, it elicits some exuberant and insightful connections to the literature.

Enrichment

Have students incorporate a minimum of two visuals into the performance of the poems.

Robert Kohser

Evaluating Irony

Type of activity: Individual. Approximate time: One 50-minute class period.

Objective

Students will learn to understand and recognize irony, will identify the use of irony in popular culture, and will discover the delicate skill of using irony effectively in writing.

Materials

An overhead projector; a CD or cassette of Alanis Morissette's song, "Ironic"; transparencies of the lyrics to the song; a CD or cassette player to play the song; and pen and paper, or computer with word processor.

Set-Up

Have the overhead set up with the lyrics to "Ironic," as well as the song itself ready on CD or tape. Students will need two sheets of paper.

Procedure

The students should first be instructed to write the word "Irony" on the top of one sheet of paper. Discuss the word briefly, elicit and talk about definitions, and all students will write an appropriate definition for the word. Once this has been accomplished, play the song and show the lyrics, line by line as they are played. After the song has been played all the way through, instruct all students to write five of the examples in the song that were "ironic." Most students will remember five of them easily, and once everyone has written the examples, hold a discussion and comparison session. Next, instruct students to come up with five examples of irony that were not evident in the song. Once again, hold a short discussion and comparison, noting the different examples chosen as being ironic.

Once discussion has concluded, all students should choose one of the examples of irony from their list and write a poem or short story about it. Writing these poems or stories should take up the remainder of the class, leaving only enough time for students to read their irony poems aloud.

Summary

Three months after this activity, my twelfth graders are still talking about irony and showing enthusiasm in identifying it. Alanis Morissette's song is a popular one that most students will have heard at one time or another, and many will sing along as it is played. *One word of caution: The lyrics do contain the word* damn *in them, which is something to consider in a more conservative community or with younger students.*

Enrichment

Some of the more astute students will take notice that not all of Morissette's examples of irony are truly ironic. This makes for an excellent opportunity to open the floor for discussion of which examples from the song were the good examples of irony and which ones were not. This could be taken as far as having students number the examples in order of which ones were best to which ones were weakest. Many students will welcome a chance to compare their sense of irony to a classmate's. Usually, much debate ensues with students relying on close textual analysis for support.

Clarissa West-White

Overcoming Adversity

Type of activity: Group multimedia. Approximate time: 2 to 3 days.

Objective

Students will raise their reading abilities and performance skills via a play adaptation.

Materials

Pearl Buck's *The Big Wave* (1986), current events from local newspaper, movie clips, camcorder, television, VCR, posters, and markers (material for sets).

Set-up

Hold discussions, sponsor formal debates, and view films that deal with overcoming adversities. Have students share personal adversities they have overcome.

Procedure

After sparking their interest, the class read *The Big Wave*. Buck's play is an excellent example of people overcoming adversity and a way to incorporate several lessons in one. After reading the play orally so that students get a feel for it, assign parts, and ask students to act it out in front of a video camera. After their taped reenactment, divide students into groups of two and ask them to create their own plays with the understanding that they will be videotaped. The class will then discuss the final products in a workshop and choose the best plays to perform. Decide the casts for all plays at once. Students should volunteer for the characters they wish to play until a consensus is reached. Once the cast is chosen, students have the right as "actors" to ad lib or change the script.

Tape each performance and ask the performing group collectively to create a quiz to accompany their video. After viewing the taped plays, ask the remaining groups to point out what adversity had been overcome and the play's moral, as well as offer suggestions for plot development. Give each group's quiz to spark class discussion.

Summary

Overcoming Adversity teaches far more than simple punctuation, capitalization, acts, and scenes, and it goes far beyond simply mimicking Buck's play. Students have to use numerous skills in order to put their final products together. Not only do they write, proofread, edit, critique, and perform in front of live audiences, but they also create a quiz that exercises their critical thinking and problem-solving skills. Students learn that they are often more creative than they first thought, and rely on cooperation in designing scenes and deciding which plays are the best. Those students who are not as academically successful as some of their classmates, are able to display their intelligences.

Enrichment

Have students research historic and media figures who have overcome adversity. Ask students if a prerequisite of greatness is the ability to overcome adversity. If so, to what extent? Have students create a chart of the characteristics a person must have in order to "make it." You may want to discuss parts of D.K. Simonton's book *Greatness: Who Makes History and Why* (1999).

Assessment

The grading rubric I have used encourages students to include as many scenes and to participate in as much of the production as possible to achieve the best grade. Those who complete a play, regardless of length or format, receive an Average (C). Those who want to aim higher know that in order to earn Above Average (B) or Excellent (A), they will have to include more than one scene and a narrator part; have more than four characters and a clear antagonist or protagonist; include terms such as *fade to, open on, go to*; act in a number of plays; and take on other roles when not "on screen." For creating the quiz, students also may earn five points to add to a previous lower grade.

LITERATURE

OVERCOMING ADVERSITY STUDENT SAMPLE

THURSDAY

Characters:

Nyesha   Brian
Robin   Miric
Maria   Coach
Narrator

Scene One

Open on: A scene in Detroit, Michigan, at Detroit High School. Nyesha and her brother Brian arrive to their first day of school after moving there from Florida and already have enemies.

Nyesha: Hello everyone, nice to meet you all. [Nyesha continues walking past the two girls at a nearby bench and sits.]

Robin: Who was that girl?

Maria: Oh, that's Nyesha.

Robin: Nyesha who?

Maria: I don't know her last name. All I know is that she's from Miami.

Robin: Maria, lets go meet her. Let's see how Miami girl is.

Maria: Okay.

Narrator: Robin and Maria walk over to where Nyesha was sitting and started the conversation by introducing themselves. Maria and Robin thought Nyesha was going to be scared of them, but she wasn't. Nyesha stood her ground and let the girls know that she would not kiss up to them. Robin and Maria liked what they saw in her, and they quickly became good friends.

Scene Two

Open on: The school's football field. Brian is there trying out for the varsity football team.

Coach: Alright boys! This year our football team is going to be number one because we are going to work hard and get it right.

Brian: Excuse me! Excuse me!

Coach: Yes? Are you here to tryout, son?

(continued)

OVERCOMING ADVERSITY STUDENT SAMPLE (continued)

Brian: Yes, I really had my heart set on playing football again this year after the middle school I played with came in third at state last year, but my parents' jobs transferred them here. Do you have any positions up for grab?

Coach: Maybe, we will have to see. As I was saying....

Narrator: A voice comes up behind Brian. It is Miric, the captain of the football team and also the captain of the boy's basketball team.

Miric: You are a freshman, right? And you say you're here to tryout? That's funny! [He laughs.]

Brian: Yes, I am a freshman and I come to try out for the football team, unless you're scared I'm gonna take your place.

Miric: Boy, you're fresh meat now, but when I get through with you, you're going to be spoiled meat.

Brian: It ain't no thang, let's see if you can hang.

Narrator: They start sprinting up the sideline to see who can run the 40 faster.

Scene Three
[Fade to: The girl's are in class, talking.]

Maria: Well, Nyesha how long are you going to be here?

Nyesha: Until my brother and I finish school.

Robin: How old is your brother?

Nyesha: He's fifteen.

Robin: Girl, you're gonna have to introduce us to him.

Maria: What's his name?

Nyesha: His name is Brian, and I would introduce you to him today after school, but he is staying after for football practice. I will be staying after too because I am trying out for the basketball team.

Maria: Nyesha, haven't you heard? We only have a boy's basketball team.

Robin: Why won't you try out for cheerleading with Maria and me?

Nyesha: I am going to try out for the basketball team and that's all there is to it!

Narrator: Nyesha tries out and makes the basketball team. Brian makes the football team and is now the starting QB.

The End

Anthony Kunkel

Crossing Edson's Bridge

**Type of activity: Individual.
Approximate time: Two to three
class periods.**

Objective

Students will learn to analyze rhetorical techniques, will gain creative writing skills; and will identify imagery; metaphors, and figurative language within selected writing.

Materials

The short story, "The Bridge," by Russell Edson. (See handout on page 142.)

Set-Up

None needed.

Procedure

STEP ONE

Instruct students to read "The Bridge," and to write a well-constructed essay, analyzing and discussing the imagery and metaphors used by Edson in his story. One class period should be plenty of time for this step to be accomplished.

STEP TWO

Collect and redistribute all essays so that no student has his or her own writing. Instruct students to analyze and score their peer's essay, paying close attention to how well it is constructed and how well the imagery and metaphors are discussed. Provide a rubric based on the level of the class and your expectations during this step.

STEP THREE

After discussing Edson's story and the metaphors and imagery found within, ask students to write a sequel to the story, beginning with the character having just "crossed the bridge." Students should attempt to model Edson's prose style and tone, striving to incorporate new imagery and metaphors. They also should pay close attention to the length of their sequel.

Summary

This lesson was designed for my eleventh-grade Advanced Placement classes, but I have adapted it for basic ninth-grade classes as well. The results have produced some terrific student writing. I always try habit to allow time for students who want to read their stories aloud.

Enrichment

This activity is an excellent set-up for a unit on reading comprehension. Students not only become active readers, but do so as critical writers. Having students do a second essay that analyzes the various stories that were produced in class changes the atmosphere from writing the traditional essay on selected reading to reading critically as a peer reviewer.

THE BRIDGE
by Russell Edson

In his travels he comes to a bridge made entirely of bones. Before crossing he writes a letter to his mother: Dear mother, guess what? the ape accidentally bit off one of his hands while eating a banana. Just now I am at the foot of a bone bridge. I shall be crossing it shortly. I don't know if I shall find hills and valleys made of flesh on the other side, or simply constant night, villages of sleep. The ape is scolding me for not teaching him better. I am letting him wear my pith helmet for consolation. The bridge looks like one of those skeletal reconstructions of a huge dinosaur one sees in a museum. The ape is looking at the stump of his wrist and scolding me again. I offer him another banana and he gets very furious, as though I'd insulted him. Tomorrow we cross the bridge. I'll write to you from the other side if I can; if not, look for a sign....

From *Micro Fiction*, Jerome Stern (Ed.). (1996). (p. 78). New York: W.W. Norton.

CROSSING EDSON'S BRIDGE
STUDENT SAMPLE

Dear mother,

We have crossed the bone bridge. I was uncertain as to what to expect. Upon reaching the other end, we came upon a toll booth, of sorts. The guardian there was a serious, stone-faced man. He demanded to know our purpose in coming, or what we intended to do if we were permitted to pass. I had to admit that I didn't quite know. It was merely dependent upon what we found across the way. Of course, being unable to tell this, as we might be denied passage, I made up a frivolous excuse, which, after some contemplation, the guardian grudgingly accepted. Descending the steps of the bridge, I looked out at the world around me. I had guessed right on one account, it was full of flesh; that is, people everywhere. It seemed a happy place after the bridge of bones. Th ape shrieked behind me. He must see something I don't. I gave him my helmet to satisfy him for awhile, then continued on. I will write more later…

Tracie Pullum

Letter to Olaudah

Type of activity: Individual.
Approximate time: 4 days.

Objective

Students will recognize Olaudah's story as a true account of a kidnapped African, will understand the conditions under which Africans were brought to America, and will write a friendly letter using the correct format.

Materials

Thomas, V.M. *Lest we forget.* (1997). New York: Crown Publishers.
Equiano, O. & Carretta, V. (Ed.). (1995). *The interesting narrative and other writings.* New York: Penguin.
Overhead projector and transparency of friendly letter format.
Copies of format for friendly letter (unlabeled).
Border paper (see student sample).

Procedure

Day One

Ask students to freewrite from the following prompt: What do you think it was like for Africans to be taken into slavery and shipped to a new unknown place? What did they go through? How were they treated? How did they feel?

Share the book *Lest We Forget* by viewing, reading, and discussing it with the class.

Days Two and Three: Minilesson on Writing a Friendly Letter

Discuss and label the different parts of the friendly letter using an overhead and the unlabeled copies of the friendly letter.

As a class read a slave narrative, then discuss and compare it with *Lest We Forget*.

Students will write a friendly letter to Olaudah Equiano from any point of view they want: as a student learning about him, as another slave on the ship, as an African he knew before he left Africa, or as a slave during slavery. Students may want to write their letters in dialect. Students must show proof that they have learned something about slavery in their letter.

LETTER TO OLAUDAH STUDENT SAMPLE

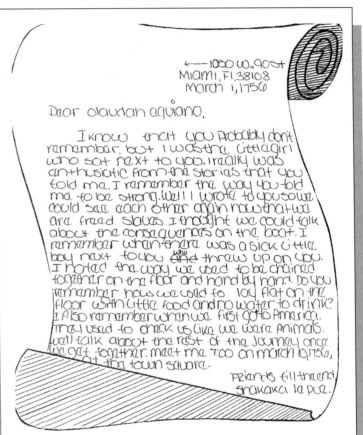

Day Four

Have students meet with a partner to see if punctuation, grammar, and spelling are correct, while you float to read their work and assist with corrections. When revisions are complete, tell students to write a final draft of their letter on border paper and cut it out.

Summary

Students are usually interested and stunned to hear and read about slavery issues. The book *Lest We Forget* is a great attention grabber with its copies of actual documents and photographs. Many students and parents have told me that they have purchased the book since its introduction in my class. In general, students are eager to write to Olaudah and seem to enjoy the freedom of point of view and voice in creating their letter. Besides learning the correct format for writing a letter (a skill that is not often taught to adolescents), the students demonstrate that they learn a few facts about slavery and gain a certain understanding of the historical period.

LITERATURE

In poetry, you must love the words, the ideas and the images and rhythms with all your capacity to love anything at all.

Stevens, W. (1990). *Opus posthumous.* New York: Vintage Press.

It…purges from our inward sight the film of familiarity which obscures from us the wonder of our being. It compels us to feel that which we perceive, and to imagine that which we know.

Shelley, P.B. (1990). A defense of poetry. In M. Stephens (Ed.), *Collins dictionary of literary quotations* (pp. 104–108). Glasgow, Scotland: HarperCollins. (Original work published 1820)

POETRY

AN EXPERIENCE YOU HAD WITH A YOUNG WOMAN IN YOUR JUNIOR ENGLISH CLASS a few years ago has given you a healthy skepticism about teaching poetry. She wrote a poem about how being away from her 16-year-old boyfriend was like living in a desert. "I'm thirsty, I'm thirsty, I'm thirsty…for your kiss." It was a sweet sentiment, though a bit clichéd and she seemed overly fond of ellipsis. Later in the poem, she began using other kinds of metaphors—a pillow, a glove, a meal, and even a flower. That would have been fine, but she kept repeating the "I'm thirsty…" refrain (always with the ellipsis), so she ended up writing that she was "thirsty…for his arms, which fit like a glove around me," "thirsty…for his soft caress like a pillow," "thirsty…like I've gone days without steak and bread," and "thirsty…to see you make me smile like a sunflower in spring." When you tried to counsel the author with regard to word choice and internal consistency, she bristled, "You cannot grade a poem. A poem is perfect—my poem is perfect just the way that it is. It expresses exactly how I feel about my boyfriend."

Activity	Entry point	Students work on	Preparation time needed
Reflective Research	Students share personal fact	Research, poetry writing	Substantial
Onomatopoeic Poems	Image	Onomatopoeia	Substantial
Anglo-Saxon Riddles	Riddles	Thinking analytically	Minimal
Soul and Sense	Autobiographical writing	Adding sensory details	Minimal
Poetry Posse	Contemporary song	Writing poetry	Substantial

Of course, you love poetry—you're an English teacher, after all. The only problems with poetry are that students often have very negative attitudes about it, no one makes a living out of writing it, and with the growing acceptance of free verse and found poetry, anything and everything seems to constitute a poem these days. As an English teacher, you used to become anguished when you read about activities that advocated making poems out of the text of newspaper articles by simply shifting punctuation marks. That was editing—not poetry. Tennyson, Whitman, Dunbar, and Plath wrote poetry.

Despite your sometimes negative experiences with teaching poetry, you realize that nothing inculcates in students the love of the language and the significance of word choice better than reading and writing poems. So you teach poetry as a fun activity in which students get to think, move around, research, experiment with language, and perform poetry as if it still mattered. It still does.

Clarissa West-White

Reflective Research: Portrait and Poem

Type of activity: Individual research.
Approximate time: 2 to 3 days.

Objective

Students will use reflective writing as a springboard into a research assignment.

Materials

Access to career information and library or media center.

Set-Up

This activity can be used as the first assignment of a creative writing class and should be given after a number of introductory activities.

Procedure

Ask students to share one personal fact about themselves, then discuss similarities and differences among students in the class. Spend time on how life experiences shape who we are and who we ultimately will become. Read aloud to students an excerpt from a self-portrait, such as *Anne Frank: The Diary of a Young Girl* (1993), James Joyce's *Portrait of the Artist as a Young Man* (1992), *The Narrative of Sojourner Truth* (1993), or *The Story of My Life* (1991) by Helen Keller. Ask students to create their own self-portraits, following a similar format as the story you just read. Within each student's final paragraph, they must either mention where they will be in a given number of years, or what they want to do if they someday control the world. Out of this activity grows the research poem. Their assignment is then to search for facts on a topic, career, or idea out of the final paragraph of their portrait. The top half of their final word-processed document should include their factual statements, and the lower portion should consist of the poem that evolved from their research.

Summary

This assignment allows you to get to know your students on a rather personal level and to learn of their dreams. You will learn what their interests are, which will help you to plan accordingly for the class. More importantly, you may learn what makes each student behave a certain way and know how to deal effectively with students if they misbehave.

Students should be able to have fun writing their portraits without worrying so much about grammar. Not only is this a good chance for you to see each student's writing ability, sentence formation, and writing style, you also will be able to witness students smiling and sharing their work with their neighbors; these same students who stated during the introductory activities that they hated writing or that writing was boring. Students will become more familiar with themselves, and although this familiarization cannot be measured on a test, knowing oneself is as important as scoring in the 99th percentile. The second part of this activity tests students' research skills and their ability to condense information. It will also help you to gauge which students are more creative and which are more analytical or naturalistic. Students should employ a variety of strategies for gaining information, and many will gain valuable information about a career or issue.

Assessment

These assignments should be assessed with two separate grades. Those who simply completed the self-portrait receive 100 points. The research half of the research poem is worth 50 points, and the actual poem is worth the remaining 50 points. The majority of my grading policies have been designed so that students clearly understand that I am more concerned with quality, effort, and growth than with quantity. My ultimate mission is to make writing an enjoyable reflective process.

REFLECTIVE RESEARCH STUDENT SAMPLE

SELF PORTRAIT

When I was born, Ellanor and Sylvester Hatten were the proud parents of a ten-pound, five-ounce baby girl. Although my parents had me at the age of 17, they were still happy to have me. I was born on August 6, 1982, in the Sawdust Community area. When I was two months old, I had to live with my father's mother, Jesse Mae Hatten. My grandmother raised me for two years after I was born. She did this because at the time of my birth, my parents were not financially stable. They were living in a one-bedroom, one-bathroom house in which a small child could simply not be raised.

By the time I was six years old, another child had been added to the family. I no longer was an only child. On October 28, 1988, my parents gave birth to another girl. They named her LaToya Cherie Hatten. I can remember when my parents brought her home from the hospital, and how excited I was to have a little sister to boss around. Then two years later, my parents finally had the baby boy they always wanted. They named him Sylvester Lee Hatten Jr. By now, we had lived in five different houses in a period of only four years.

When I turned thirteen, my body, as well as, my school had changed. I was no longer a child, but a young lady. At this age I started to develop breasts, hips, and my femininity. Also, I began attending Greensboro High School as a seventh grader. I was very scared my first day because I didn't know anybody or anything. As the years progressed I learned many interesting things about school and life.

Now that I am fifteen, I am a sophomore at Greensboro High School. Being at this school helped me to learn more about others and myself. I am currently a member of the Student Government Association, Beta Club, Culture Club, and Key Club. I am also president of the sophomore class, an honor student, and member of Salter's Angels. I am also a scorekeeper for varsity volleyball. During my three years of at-

(continued)

POETRY

REFLECTIVE RESEARCH STUDENT SAMPLE (continued)

tendance at Greensboro High, I have accomplished many things and I am very proud of myself.

When I am older, I do not want to be in charge of the world. I would like to become an attorney at a law firm in Georgia. I hope to have three children and to be married. I also hope to remain saved and to live a Christian life. If I were to be in charge, everyone would be saved, and we would have no more wars or homelessness. Also, I would discover a cure for cancer and AIDS. But, for right now, I am just taking matters one day at a time and trying to live a good Christian life to its fullest.

Research Poetry

- AIDS is a disease that has no cure.
- AIDS is a disease that come from the virus HIV.
- Some people think that the disease started with the green monkeys.
- AIDS is a deadly disease.
- Anyone can get AIDS.
- You can only get AIDS through sexual intercourse, sharing of needles, or through a blood transfusion.
- HIV can be passed through breast feeding from an infected mother to her baby.
- You cannot catch AIDS from social kissing, hugging, and sneezing.
- You can survive AIDS by abstinence.
- The first known case involved a homosexual man and a drug abuser.

AIDS

AIDS is a disease that has no cure.
AIDS is a disease that is strong and makes you insecure.

AIDS was first found in a homosexual man,
now it can happen to any human.

Some people think that it came from green monkeys,
others believe that it started with drug abusers and junkies.

You can get AIDS through sexual intercourse,
but you can choose abstinence, because its your choice.

AIDS is a disease that can be passed to your unborn baby, which should drive us, as a society, crazy!

AIDS is a disease that you can catch from anywhere, but it is not a disease that you can get from playing in someone's hair.

AIDS is a disease that should be approached with caution, it causes death and sadness to many, often.

Mike Rychlik

Onomatopoeic Poems

Type of activity: Small groups of two or three students.
Approximate time: One or two class periods.

Objective

Students will comprehend and identify onomatopoeia, use this literary device in collaborative writing, and perform a choral reading of an original poem.

Materials

Overhead transparencies and markers or chalk and chalkboard.

Copies of Isabella Stewart Gardner's poem "Summer Remembered" (see page 156 for complete poem).

Set-Up

Have a transparency or write onomatopoeic words on the board to show prepared examples of words that sound like what they mean (see Figure 1).

Read Isabella Stewart Gardner's poem and discuss imagery.

FIGURE 1

Onomatopoeic Words
Sound Like What They Mean

plump	crash	hiss
swoosh	chomp	sizzle
clink		crunch
snap	bloop	toot
plop	tap	buzz
slurp		crackle

Procedure

After reading Gardner's poem, have students each create a list of words that the poem brings to mind. Students should then be allowed to abandon their word list and follow their instincts, if they are so inclined.

Set time limits on each step of the activity. For instance, give the groups 2 minutes to brainstorm other words, then have them tally their words up as if it were a competition. Then have the students pass their list to the group on the left so that each list circulates around the room. At this point, tell students to add as many words as they can on another sheet of paper during each transfer-and-share session; friendly competition motivates the students. A 1-minute time limit keeps the activity moving and keeps the students thinking quickly. At the end of the brainstorm, ask each group to report how many total onomatopoeia words they've accumulated in their "word bank." Put the transparency of storm images (see Figure 2 on page 155) on the overhead, and have each group of students create onomatopoeia words with each image. Once each group reports its findings, collectively read "Summer Remembered." Following a brief discussion about the poem's usage of onomatopoeia to create sensory images, instruct the students to compose a group poem consisting of a minimum of eight lines and four onomatopoeic sound words. Each group will be required to collectively read their poem to the class.

FIGURE 2

USE ONOMATOPOEIC WORDS TO DESCRIBE THESE SOUNDS

the sound of a thunderstorm

wind blowing through the trees

a person walking through the mud

glass breaking

water dripping from a roof

an outdoor electrical line breaking

logs burning in a fireplace

an old radio tuned into an AM station

emergency sirens in the distance

Summary

This is a highly interactive, fun activity that can produce many positive results. Initially, the students really enjoy the competitive nature of the prewriting exercises. They also tend to become fascinated by the mystery of the assignments as they unfold. In other words, a lot of their enthusiasm is derived from their willingness to "experience" the activity as it jumps from one stage to the next. Most surprisingly, however, are the final products. The students will write some really nice poems full of sound imagery, and their oral deliveries are usually dramatic.

Enrichment

In extension, the students could collect actual sounds that emulate the onomatopoeic devices in the poems. The sounds can be recorded from sound-effect sources or self-made while the students reads their poems.

SUMMER REMEMBERED

by Isabella Stewart Gardner

Sounds sum and summon the remembering of sum-
    mers.
The humming of the sun
The mumbling in the honey-suckle vine
The whirring in the clovered grass
The pizzicato plinkle of ice in an auburn uncle's am-
    ber glass.

From Gardner, I.S. (1990). *Isabella Gardner: The collected poems.* New York: Boa.

POETRY

Alan Perry

Anglo-Saxon Riddles

SECTION 9

Type of activity: Individual.
Approximate time: 1 day.

Objective

Students will learn how to create riddles and will think analytically.

Materials

A class set of copies of the Anglo-Saxon riddle poems "Shield" and "Iceberg" published in the *Exeter Book Riddles*. (See page 158 for these poems.)

Set-Up

Hand out copies of the riddle poems to the students and have them read them.

Procedure

The Anglo-Saxons typically wrote riddles about subjects with which they were familiar. Instruct students to write their own riddle poems using an object that they might find at home, school, or elsewhere as a subject. They should make their riddle poem's title the subject of their riddle; also, encourage them to write it in the style of the Old English riddle poems.

Summary

Anglo-Saxon riddle poems have been around for hundreds of years. Writing these riddles forces students to think in highly analytic and creative ways.

Enrichment

Read the poems aloud without revealing their titles, and have the entire class guess the subject of each student's riddle poem.

POETRY

Anglo-Saxon Riddle Poems

The Anglo-Saxons of England loved riddles and often made them up in the form of poems. Ninety-four such riddles were found in the *Exeter Book*. Below are two of the poems that were published there:

Shield

I am a lonely warrior, wounded by iron,
Stricken by a sword, weary of battle-works,
Tired of blades. Oft I see combat,
Fighting a brave foe, I cannot expect comfort,
Safety to come to me in saving struggle,
Before I perish entirely among men;
But the leavings of hammers strike me,
The hard-edged, battle-sharp handiwork of smiths,
Bites me in the stronghold. I must await
A more hateful encounter. Never a physician
Could I find on the battlefield,
One who with herbs might heal my wounds;
But the blows of the swords grow greater
Through death-strokes, by day and by night.

Iceberg

A creature came travling, wondrous along the waves,
It called out in comeliness from ship to land,
Loud was its din; terrible its laughter,
Dreadful on earth; sharp were its edges.
It was fierce in malice, in battle too sluggish,
Bitter in battle-deeds, wooden walls it shattered,
Cruel and ravaging. It spread about a baleful charm;
It spoke with cunning about its own nature:
"My mother is among maidens the dearest,
She is my daughter grown to greatness,
As is known to men among the people,
She shall stand with joy on the earth everywhere."

The Anglo-Saxons wrote riddles mainly about subjects with which they were familiar. Write your own riddle poem using as a subject an object you might find in your home, school, or elsewhere. Make your riddle poem's title the subject of your riddle; write it in the style of the Old English ones. We'll see if your classmates can guess the subject of your riddles.

Riddles from Crossley-Holland, K. (1993). *The Exeter book riddles.* New York: Penguin.

Lawrence Baines

Soul and Sense Poetry

Type of activity: Begins individually, evolves into a cooperative writing assignment, then ends with the creation of an individual poem. Approximate time: 50 minutes.

Objective

Students will use words that appeal to the five senses to describe themselves, their dispositions, and their values and will learn to improve the precision of their descriptions.

Materials

Pen and paper or a computer with a word-processing program.

Set-Up

Have students write a list of words that describe both their "inner" and "outer" selves. This usually takes about 10 minutes.

Ask students if they believe that humans have souls. What does a soul look like? What does it sound like? (If some students seem uncomfortable with the term *soul*, allow them to substitute *attitude* or *outlook on life*.) Next, tell students that they are going to describe their souls, attitudes, or outlooks on life by describing themselves, their accomplishments, appearance, likes, and dislikes through the five senses—smell, taste, touch, sight, and hearing.

Write a set of descriptive words on the board as an example: *happy, sloppy, skinny, athletic, tennis player, brother, likes tie-dye T-shirts*. Identify that some words on the board, such as *happy, sloppy, skinny, athletic* are adjectives; other words, such as *tennis player* and *brother* are nouns; *likes tie-dye T-shirts* is a phrase. Tell students that all the parts of speech are acceptable in creating their initial lists.

Next ask students which of the words on the board specifically appeal to one of the five senses.

Most students will acknowledge that most of the words seem to appeal to a sense of sight or to no sense at all. Write this list on the board:

Happy - smell - ?

Sloppy - taste - ?

Skinny - touch - ?

Athletic - sight - ?

Tennis player - sound - ?

Tell students to give a concrete example of how each word could be described through a particular sense. For example, a happy smell might be freshly buttered popcorn or cotton candy. A sloppy taste might be eating a huge taco with one hand while you are trying to drive a car down a busy freeway.

Have students "sensitize" their self-descriptions by attempting to connect words with one of the five senses as mentioned earlier. For this part of the activity, allow students to join up with others in groups of three or four. If possible, allow students to choose their own groups, but no group should contain more than four members.

Procedure

Students should not show others in their group their lists.

One member of the group is the focus of every group member's writing for 5 to 8 minutes. Students should attempt to describe aspects of the person with which they are familiar by first generating lists of words, then going back and sensitizing their list. While other members of the group write lists of words that describe the student in focus, or the focus student takes out the original self-made list and adds to it. After time has elapsed, tell each member of the group to give their list to the person who was the focus for writing. The focus rotates until each student has lists from all members of the group.

Each student may draw from any of these lists as he or she writes a poem that describes his or her soul, attitude, or outlook on life. The poem may be rhyming or nonrhyming.

Summary

In addition to allowing students to discover how others feel about them, Soul and Sense Poetry gets students to think in novel ways about words and the myriad levels on which words can communicate. Soul and Sense Poetry is very useful for classes of students who have yet to venture much beyond long lists of adjectives in their descriptive writing.

Enrichment

A wonderful exercise is to allow students to make short videos of their Soul and Sense Poetry. Through video, students can mix images, music, words, and sounds to construct a unique, highly personal statement.

SOUL AND SENSE POETRY STUDENT SAMPLES

My soul is ghostly white
looks like a fog at night
sounds like the whistling wind
coming 'round the darkly-lit bend.
Smells like tomato plants
but tastes like chocolate covered ants
feels like evaporating dew
nobody knew
what it has been through.

Not many have seen
my soul pink, yellow, and green
he hides inside of me
small as a flea.
But he can grow the size of the earth
at old age or birth
my soul makes lots of noise
loud as the Beastie Boys
tastes like chocolate sundae
any day...
My soul would smell like fresh air
never stink, God, I swear
would feel like a cloud
soft, but not a shroud
a snow white pillow soft as cotton
when it feels good, it's rotten.

My soul is a pink glow, low and soft
kind of flickering as if it's about to
   go out,
a low murmur, indistinctive, afraid
   to burst out,
channel #9 after a long day, worn
   away
with only a hint of fragrance to stay.
Sweet like ice cream but more like
   cuisine
not strong or spicy but tempting.
Like satin soft, but quick to wear
   away
easily soiled or hurt
winding down the day.

Barbara Moore

Poetry Posse

Type of activity: Individual and cooperative groups.
Approximate time: 1 hour; can be divided into segments.

Objective

Students will use expressive and figurative language to create vivid word pictures and make connections with words to define and imaginatively describe images and feelings of living in the world.

Materials

Pen or pencil and paper or a computer with a word-processing program.

Set-Up

Read the words from a contemporary piece of music (poetry), which may need editing, depending on age level, without revealing the author. Ask students if they can identify the author (usually, they cannot without the music). Then, play the music and ask them to determine the poet or songwriter. One of my favorite songs for this activity is "The One" by Elton John. This particular piece also provides several examples of similes and metaphors. You also can use a piece of music that pertains to a specific subject you may be targeting for publication. For example, I also read and played "Circle of Life," by Elton John, after we discussed our purpose for writing—an Earth anthology and play performance. "Hero," by Maria Carey and "The Rose," by Bette Midler are also good song choices for this activity.

Collect as many books or author examples of poetry and prose as possible (Frost, Poe, Browning, Sandburg, Keats, Silverstein, Bible psalms). Examine and discuss various forms, formats, and styles of poetry.

Determine a purpose for writing. Most age levels of students can relate to protecting our environment, and students respond well to writing about the Earth. (We decided we had plenty of things to say about our planet and what we particularly liked about it. We also had a desire to publish our pieces collectively. In ad-dition, we wanted to share our love of our home in space to others as part of a play.)

Define your criteria for the project, which could be used as part of an assessment rubric:

1. Use similes and metaphors to make compar-isons.
2. Express feelings and images through word pictures.
3. Take ownership in group production—team-work.
4. Go through the writing process.
5. Share.

Brainstorm (prewrite) together a list or web about Earth concerns and what the class loves most about it.

Then, write a simple poem together using simi-les and metaphors.

Procedure

Take the class for a walk outside: smell the flow-ers, crunch the leaves, hug a tree, feel the rocks, and lay on the ground and watch the clouds and world go by for several minutes. If possible, have students stay outside and write (list or web) random thoughts about what they saw, smelled, touched, heard, and felt. You could also let students dance to a music (poetry) sam-ple. Celebrating poetry through music allows another chance to experience the joy in writing—poetry in motion.

Students should write rough drafts independently. Emphasize the enjoyment of writing poetry about something we care about—quantity, not quality—as long as it comes from the heart.

Once rough drafts are written, briefly meet with students to talk about what's good and what could be revised in their poems. Split class into small groups and have students revise in peer conferences, partner-read for sense, practice expressive reading, and self-check for the assignment criteria.

Publish students' final drafts in a class poetry anthology, and share the anthology with other classes and grades.

Summary

Students often enter negatively into the concept of poetry. Using familiar music and nature walks are excellent springboards to the realization that poetry is really all around them. This lesson develops self-confidence, listening, speaking, reading, and writing skills. Additionally, you can require specific language arts components (in this case, use of similes and metaphors) into the project. However, the freedom of "anything goes" as far as form and content allows the real purpose of this exercise to be realized: the joy of writing poetry from the heart.

Enrichment

Compile individual poems into a collection for publication.

Host a "coffee house" style reading for invited guests, or have students read poetry as part of a play. For example, one of my students read during the intermission of an Earth Day play performed by second graders, and "angel" poetry was presented by another student during a Christmas performance.

POETRY

Appendix

Resources

Books

Andrews, L. (1993). *Language exploration and awareness*. White Plains, NY: Longman.

Buck, P. (1986). *The big wave*. New York: HarperTrophy.

Burroway, J. (1987). *Writing fiction*. Boston: Little, Brown.

Cawelti, G. (Ed.). (1995). *Handbook of research on improving student achievement*. Arlington, VA: Educational Research Service.

Chandler, R. (1995). *Stories and early novels*. New York: Library of America.

Crossley-Holland, K. (1993). *The Exeter Book riddles*. New York: Penguin.

Dickens, C. (1995). *A christmas carol*. New York: Bantam.

Doyle, A.C. (1998). *The complete Sherlock Holmes: All 4 novels and 56 short stories*. New York: Bantam Doubleday Dell.

Farrell, E., & Miller, J. (Eds.). (1997). *The perceptive I*. Lincolnwood, IL: National Textbook.

Faulkner, W. (1987). A rose for Emily. In L. Fowler, G. Walker, & K. McCormick (Eds.), *The Lexington introduction to literature* (pp. 253–259). Lexington, KY: D.C. Heath & Company.

Frank, A. (1993). *Anne Frank: Diary of a young girl*. New York: Bantam Doubleday Dell.

Gardner, I.S. (1990). *Isabella Gardner: The collected poems.* New York: Boa.

Gardner, J. (1985). *The art of fiction.* New York: Vintage.

Grisham, J. (1997). *The rainmaker.* New York: Doubleday.

Grafton, S. (1997). *M is for malice.* New York: Henry Holt.

Green, R., & Love-Carroll, D. (1996). *A salute to black pioneers.* New York: Empak.

Green, R. (1986). *A salute to historic black women.* New York: Empak.

Hemingway, E. (1990). *The complete short stories of Ernest Hemingway.* New York: Scribners.

Henry, O. (1995). *Selected stories by O. Henry.* Lincolnwood, IL: NTC Publishing.

Johnson, L., & Perry, C. (1992). *Harriet Tubman.* New York: Empak.

Joyce, J. (1992). *Portrait of the artist as a young man.* New York: Bantam.

Keller, H. (1991). *The story of my life.* New York: Doubleday.

MacKie, W.S., & Gollancz, I. (Eds.). (1995). *Exeter Book: Poems 1-VIII (Early English Text Society Series).* London: Periodicals Service Co.

Masters, E.L. (1992). *Spoon river anthology.* New York: Dover.

Moffet, J. (1983). *Teaching the universe of discourse.* Boston: Houghton Mifflin.

Mortimer, J. (1990). *Rumpole a la carte.* New York: Penguin.

National Center for Education Statistics. (1998). *The condition of education 1998.* Washington, DC: U.S. Government Printing Office.

Olaudah, E., & Carretta, V. (Eds.). (1996). *The interesting narrative and other writings.* New York: Penguin

Pelham, J. (Ed.) (1998). *Suddenly.* Houston, TX: Martin House Publishers.

Poe, E.A. (1966). The bells. In *Complete stories and poems of Edgar Allan Poe* (pp. 954–957). New York: Doubleday.

Pynchon, T. (1997). *Mason & Dixie.* New York: Henry Holt.

Ransom, J.C. (1924). *Chills and fever.* New York: Knopf.

Salinger, J.D. (1991). *The catcher in the rye.* New York: Little, Brown.

Shapard, R., & Thomas, J. (Eds.). (1986). *Sudden fiction.* Layton, UT: Gibbs Smith.

Shapard, R., & Thomas, J. (Eds.). (1989). *Sudden fiction international.* New York: W.W. Norton.

Simonton, D.K. (1999). *Greatness: Who makes history and why.* New York: Guilford.

Spillane, M. (1993). *Kiss me deadly.* New York: Macmillan.

Steinbeck, J. (1993). *Cannery row.* New York: Penguin.

Stern, J. (1991). *Making shapely fiction.* New York: Norton.

Stern, J. (Ed.). (1996). *Micro fiction.* New York: W.W. Norton.

Stevens, W. (1990). *Opus posthumous.* New York: Vintage.

Seuss, Dr. (1960). *Green eggs and ham.* New York: Random House.

Tchudi, S., & Mitchell, D. (1999). *Exploring and teaching the English language arts.* New York: Longman.

Thomas, D. (1986). *The collected stories.* New York: W.W. Norton.

Thomas, V.M. (1997). *Lest we forget.* New York: Crown.

Truth, S. (1993) *The narrative of Sojourner Truth.* New York: Vintage.

Twain, M. (1990). *The complete short stories of Mark Twain.* New York: Bantam Classic.

Magazines

National Review
Newsweek
The New Yorker
The New York Times
The Wall Street Journal
The Weekly Standard
U.S. News and World Report

Music

Barber, S. (1987). Adagio for Strings [Recorded by Janssen Symphony Orchestra, New York Philharmonic Orchestra, et al. Conducted by Leonard Bernstein.] On *Barber Adagio and Other Romantic Favorites for Strings* [compact disc]. New York: Sony Classics.

Carey, M. (1993). Hero. On *Music box* [compact disc]. New York: Sony/Columbia Records.

John, E. (1992). The one. On *The one* [compact disc]. Universal City, CA: MCA Records.

John, E., Zimmer, H., Rice, T., Weaver, J., Lane, N., Williams, J., & Sabella, E. (1994). Circle of life. On *The lion king: Original motion picture soundtrack* [compact disc]. Burbank, CA: Disney.

Midler, B. (1993). The rose. On *Experience the divine: Bette Midler greatest hits* [compact disc]. New York: Atlantic.

Morissette, A. (1995). Ironic. On *Jagged little pill* [compact disc]. Los Angeles: Warner Brothers Records.

Tabloids

The Globe
National Enquirer

Television

Pop-Up Videos on VH1 cable network

Video/Film

Granada Television. (1985). *The adventures of Sherlock Holmes: The blue carbuncle* [Film]. Starring: Jeremy Brett.

Hickox, D. (Director). (1983). *Sherlock Holmes: The hound of the Baskervilles* [Film]. Starring: Ian Richardson.

Neill, R.W. (Director). (1945). *Sherlock Holmes: The woman in green* [Film]. Starring: Basil Rathbone.

Stone, O. (Director). (1986). *Platoon* [Film]. Starring: Tom Berrenger and Charlie Sheen.